Is alchemy the quest for transforming base metals into gold? Or is it a metaphor for spiritual transformation, or else the pursuit of the elixir of eternal life? Or is it, as some people think, merely an early attempt at chemistry?

Alchemy can be as elusive as mercury, one of the chief materials that it uses. Like quicksilver, it has a shape-shifting nature, and cannot easily be pinned down to one fixed interpretation. Whatever form it takes, however, the alchemical process is one in which transformation plays a key role, and in the best traditions, this involves the soul of the alchemist as well as the material in the alchemical vessel.

In *Explore Alchemy* Cherry Gilchrist shows how alchemy has been at the heart of human wisdom from Taoist sages, through medieval Arabic magi, to heretical monks, twentieth century psychologists and modern day practitioners of the tradition. She reveals how alchemy has manifested in various ways, such as the distillation of alcohol, the invention of baroque music and the musical language of Monteverdi, the works of William Shakespeare, and the scientific insights of Sir Isaac Newton and his contemporary Robert Boyle. She provides a concise yet comprehensive guide to the complex wisdom of the alchemists.

Cherry Gilchrist read English and Anthropology at Cambridge, and holds a post-graduate diploma in Cultural Astronomy and Astrology from the University of Bath Spa. She has a wide range of interests within the areas of the hermetic tradition, ancient cultures and mythology, and she is also a specialist in Russian traditional art and culture.

Explore Alchemy

Cherry Gilchrist

The aim of Heart of Albion's 'Explore' series is to provide accessible introductions to folklore and mythology. Some books provide 'overviews' of quite broad topics, drawing together current academic research with popular beliefs. Other books in the series deal with more specific topics, but still with the aim of providing a wide-ranging introduction to the topic.

Series editor: Bob Trubshaw

Other titles in the 'Explore' series include:

Explore Folklore Bob Trubshaw

Explore Mythology Bob Trubshaw

Explore Green Men Mercia MacDermott

Explore Shamanism Alby Stone

Explore Fairy Traditions Jeremy Harte

Explore Phantom Black Dogs edited by Bob Trubshaw

Explore Hinduism Bansi Pandit

Explore Dragons Richard Freeman

Explore Vampires Bob Curran

Explore Alchemy

Cherry Gilchrist

Heart of Albion

Explore Alchemy

Cherry Gilchrist

Cover illustration:
Folio 29 from Trismosin's *Splendor Solis* of 1582.
Copyright © The British Library. All rights reserved.
Harleian Mss 3469

ISBN 97801-905646-02-9

Published by

Explore Books
an imprint of
Heart of Albion Press
2 Cross Hill Close, Wymeswold
Loughborough, LE12 6UJ

albion@indigogroup.co.uk

Visit our Web site: www.hoap.co.uk

Printed in England by Booksprint

Contents

Preface

When I was first asked to write on the subject of alchemy, in the mid-1980s, I agreed to do so with a carefree spirit. Little did I realise what complexities awaited me. My grounding in subjects such as the Cabbala, astrology, Christian mysticism and mythology was a solid one; I had actively and practically studied in this field for quite some time, and assumed that my brief excursions into alchemical literature could be padded out with no trouble at all.

This was not to be. I was both dazed and amazed by the profusion of alchemical texts, the discrepancies between them, the cryptic nature of their utterances, and the fact that no two writers on the history of alchemy ever agreed with one other. I soon came to a decision that, since I did not have a lifetime to complete the project, I would have to formulate my own way of working. This meant choosing texts of quality, according to a sense of their individual worth, and picking a new path through the jungle of alchemical history. In other words, contact with alchemy throws you back upon your own resources, and an academic training or a writer's zeal for accurate research can only take you part of the way. So it has always been; the alchemical seeker has had to work out his or her own solution to the riddles posed by the quest for gold. Like the aspiring alchemist, I was able to make use of available studies on the subject, but, ultimately, had to draw my own conclusions.

The main intention of this current book is to clarify the aims and history of alchemy, and to relate it both to other spiritual and esoteric practices, and to the arts and sciences that it influenced. In the latter category, new discoveries are frequently being made, and it is exciting to see how the symbolism and language of alchemy has affected mainstream culture. My own explorations into the links between alchemy and Baroque music form one chapter, and I have been pleased to draw upon the researches of authors like Charles Nicholl, who relates alchemy to theatre, elsewhere.

My early optimism that I would penetrate to the heart of alchemy with no problem was perhaps founded on a strong sense, which is still with me, that alchemy is in our life blood. Somehow its powerful symbolism holds a place in the collective psyche; its images occur in the dreams and fancies of people who have never read an alchemical text. In my own case, I had had experiences of dreams and spontaneous 'visions', which were revelations of the alchemical process, at a time when my own formal acquaintance with alchemy was very slight; various people have related similar experiences to me. (The great psychologist, C.G. Jung, noted the same phenomenon, which intensified his interest in alchemy as a means of psychic transmission of archetypes.) People sometimes ask if I am an alchemist: in one sense we all are – our bodies are alchemical vessels, producing extraordinary transformations from the substances that we feed them with. And anyone who has cooked supper or made a jar of jelly is in some sense an alchemist. But in the traditional sense, I have never practiced in an alchemical laboratory, only engaged with its symbols and philosophy. Perhaps something of the practicing alchemist has come down to me though. As a child, I took great delight in making an 'Aladdin's Cave' (as I thought of it) in our coal fire, using the poker to create a glowing cavern into which I tossed little scraps of every different kind of burnable substance I could find, making a kind of fiery garden full of different coloured little flames. I would watch it with wonder, and had the sense of something magical unfolding before my eyes. Unfortunately such early experiments in aesthetic alchemy were soon banned by my parents.

To my mind, alchemy is not just some quaint but outdated practice, only of historical interest. The terms by which we know it, as a tradition of lengthy laboratory work, may no longer apply, but the inner life, the dynamic process of alchemy delineated by image and symbol, can still be tapped to enliven and illuminate a number of both spiritual and practical enterprises – meditation, holistic healing, music, psychology and art, to name but a few. A study of alchemy opens up possibilities; the spirit of it still resides in human consciousness, and when we become acquainted with its language again, we can use it in our creative endeavours.

Every time that someone proclaims alchemy to be over and done with, it rises again from the ashes like the phoenix that is found among its emblems, confronting us with new possibilities, new avenues to explore. It is currently popular among psychologists and artists, and there is also a wave of contemporary alchemists who work more practically with its principles of transmutation. Likewise, in a modest way, I can claim a resurrection for my own book on the subject, which has now sprung to life again under the imprint of Heart of Albion. It has had two previous incarnations as *Alchemy: the great work*, published by Thorsons, and then as *The Elements of Alchemy* with Element Books. Each time, in a revisited and partially revised version, it has shown itself to be useful for those curious about the practice of alchemy, and a source of imaginative stimulus for readers who work with its forms and images in one way or another. This edition maintains the precedent of enabling me to revisit and partially revise the contents, and to add further illustrations. In the meantime, I have also written *Everyday Alchemy* (Rider 2002) as a practical guide to using the symbols of alchemy as a basis for personal transformation in everyday life. I have always had a sneaking feeling that alchemy has chosen me to be one of its mouthpieces, not vice versa! And it seems that the job is not quite over yet.

Cherry Gilchrist

Bath 2006

www.cherrygilchrist.co.uk

Chapter One
What is alchemy?

For several reasons, it is not an easy tradition to understand. Firstly, the chief medium of alchemical expression is through the use of mythological symbols, which are the perfect means of conveying information that can be interpreted at both a material and a spiritual level, but which defy a single and precise definition.

Secondly, alchemy's claims to produce extraordinary results in the physical world are hard to assess objectively. By the laws of science as normally understood today, it is not possible to convert other metals into gold, except by nuclear fission. But since alchemy encompasses mental as well as physical participation it inevitably goes beyond the realms of material science in its scope and may be able to produce effects on the physical level that cannot be accounted for by normal chemistry. Additionally, as we shall see, the gold produced is usually said to be quite different from ordinary gold.

Thirdly, alchemy has a history stretching back for at least two thousand years and has been practised in Eastern, Arabic and Western societies. It would be surprising indeed if it showed a uniform tradition of practice. Like any study, it has attracted many types of people with widely differing motivations. There have always been alchemists who were out-and-out materialists, greedy to try and make themselves rich by mastering the secret of creating gold. Some were merely gullible, others fraudulent, performing fake transmutations and getting their gold from the pockets of their spectators and prospective pupils rather than through any success in the laboratory. Even among the sincere and dedicated alchemists, the emphasis of approach could be very different. Some were interested more in the chemical techniques of alchemy, others in the philosophical aspects. Some saw alchemy as a path to the true meaning of Christianity, while others saw in it possibilities for producing subtle and potent medicines.

The knowledge and aim that each practitioner brought to alchemy coloured his attitude to it, and to some extent defined his mode of operation. There are certain key symbols and processes in alchemy, but no two descriptions of it are identical, which has caused many a headache for those who try and trace its history and significance. Writers on alchemy, like the alchemists themselves, define the tradition from their own view-point and inclinations. This is inevitable: there is no such thing as an 'objective' interpretation of alchemy. This should not pose a problem provided that the reader realises that a scientific, psychological or spiritual training will undoubtedly create a different emphasis in a study of alchemy, since alchemy contains all these dimensions. Few of us are likely to be equally skilled and knowledgeable on all three levels, and our personal expertise and preference will determine our approach to alchemy and our insights into its operation. Taken at its most simple level, this means that a scientist will find alchemy of interest as a form of early chemistry, the psychologist will see it as a way of mapping the human psyche through symbolic descriptions, and the mystic will interpret it as a quest for divine knowledge.

Most investigators of alchemy have produced fresh and interesting insights and interpretations, but it is worth remembering that every writer has limitations, leading us to a new and exciting viewpoint of the alchemical landscape perhaps, but often ignoring or dismissing certain key features of alchemy. The psychologist C.G. Jung, who did so much to bring the effectiveness of alchemical imagery to our attention, chose to reject the physical side of alchemy entirely. He admitted that alchemists did work in their laboratories, but stated dogmatically that 'the process never led to the desired goal' and was pursued by the alchemist only because there was nothing at the time to convince him of the senselessness of his operations. Similarly, Lynn Thorndike, an able and meticulous historian, who brought to light much fascinating material on alchemy, could not abide the use of symbol and myth in the alchemical texts, complaining that these allegories of the alchemists are insufferably tedious reading.

Alchemy demands to be taken seriously; it has been practised by men of distinction in the fields of philosophy, science, medicine and divinity who were inspired by its aims and who dedicated much time and material resources to its pursuit. In this book I have attempted to give the tradition the respect that I feel is due to it, but at the same time to highlight some of the problems of interpretation, inviting the reader

Alchemy is rich in imagery, whose symbols relate to the different elements and stages of the alchemical process. Here the double-headed dragon represents the dual poles of nature, containing sun and moon, male and female within it. (Elais Ashmole's Theatrum Chemicum Brittanicum, *1652)*

to consider their implications rather than offering simple solutions that would not do justice to the questions raised.

The name 'alchemy'

The immediate derivation of the word alchemy is from the Arabic *al kimia*. *Al* means 'the', but the meaning of the second word is not at all clear. One popular idea is that it is associated with the Egyptian word *chem*, signifying 'black' and relating to the description of Egypt as 'The Land of the Black Soil'. This would then define alchemy as 'The Egyptian Art' or 'The Black Art'. Some scholars, though, consider it more likely that the word is derived from *chyma*, a Greek word relating to the casting or fusing of metal. This in turn appears to come from *cheein*, meaning 'to pour out'; *cheein* has other variants, such as *chymos*, 'plant juice', and *chylos*, a similar word but with the added association of 'taste'. Possibly in the early days of alchemy the working of metals and the extraction of juices from plants were closely linked. (Readers who would like to investigate the etymology further are advised to read Chapter Four of *The Origins of Alchemy in Graeco-Roman Egypt* by Jack Lindsay, which is entirely devoted to this topic.)

The time-span of alchemy

The origins of alchemy cannot be precisely dated, but it emerged as an art in its own right during the last two or three centuries BC, both in the Far East (especially in China), and in Western civilization. In the West it centred on the Alexandrian culture, drawing together aspects of both the Egyptian and the classical Greek worlds. The alchemy of the East had a preoccupation with creating an elixir of longevity, while that of the Graeco-Egyptian culture dealt chiefly with metals and minerals. Both aspired to knowledge of creation and universal order; both schools fell into a decline by the fifth and sixth centuries AD. However, while the Eastern tradition carried on (with cyclical ups and downs) right through the succeeding centuries, the Western school shifted location into the Arabic world, where it was enthusiastically practised and developed until Europeans climbed back out of the 'Dark Ages' and began to take an interest in the traditions of learning that the Arabs had preserved. From the twelfth century onwards, most European countries adopted alchemy as a study in its own right. Its reputation fluctuated. Sometimes it was considered to be a most elevated study, worthy to be practised by royalty, while sometimes it was looked upon as the profession of rogues and knaves.

During the sixteenth and seventeenth centuries there was an eagerness among men of learning to gather the strands of study together, to compare and synthesise the arts, sciences, and systems of occult and divine knowledge. Triggered by the Renaissance ideal, and perpetuated by such bodies as the Rosicrucian school of philosophy, this movement gained momentum and resulted in alchemy being brought out more into the open and set alongside other disciplines. Until then, it had been treated as a secret, private study, whose knowledge was only to be passed on directly by word of mouth or through the ambiguity of symbol and allegory. As it was discussed and practised more freely, so its quality changed. Many of the principles, symbols and ideas of alchemy were incorporated into the other branches of learning, such as medicine, music and literature; alchemy itself receded from the public eye and was indeed thought extinct by many.

However, until the present day it has been practised quietly by a few adherents, and the tradition is now arousing new interest. Its imagery has shown its enduring value by finding a place in modern psychology, and the practice of a discipline that involves both scientific and psychic skills is again showing its appeal. Alchemy has reached a point of reappraisal and, reformulated, it may once again be considered a serious subject for study.

The aim of alchemy

Alchemists have always looked upon their work as a way of life, insisting that it needs dedication and sincerity of intention if it is to produce any results. They speak of it in such terms as 'our sacred philosophy', the 'work of wisdom', the 'Great Work', and the 'divine activity'. The term 'our' is used freely in alchemical texts ('our gold', 'our mercury', 'our work', etc), implying, not possessiveness, but a special alchemical form of substances and secret methods of preparation that were understood only by the true practitioners and not by outsiders. It was a way of distinguishing alchemy from ordinary pharmacy and metal-working, but it also had the effect of suggesting the existence of an exclusive band of initiates who had access to knowledge denied to ordinary mortals. While this made it clear that alchemy was more than a material craft, such secrecy also helped to induce the envy and ridicule that has dogged alchemists throughout the centuries.

The fundamental aim of alchemy was the production of the Philosopher's Stone, also known as the Elixir, or Tincture. The proof of the Stone was that it would turn a base metal into gold. Thus the transmutation into gold was seen as a mark of success, but the power lay in the Stone itself, which was the transmuting agent. It is easy for these two elements to become confused in the interpretation of alchemy, and even the alchemical texts themselves are not always clear on this point. The Stone is usually said to have something of the nature of gold in itself; it is the active element that was thought to accelerate the natural process of perfection in material. (Gold, as we shall see, was said to grow from base metals within the earth, and alchemical transmutation was therefore a speeded-up process of evolution.) The gold it could produce, however, was frequently said to be quite different from ordinary gold, being a more perfect form, and was accordingly called by such terms as 'our gold', 'exalted gold' or 'the gold of the Sages'.

The Stone was not usually described as stone-like in substance, but more often referred to as a powder or wax that could also be rendered into a liquid form, which corresponds better with its other appellations of Tincture or Elixir. Its power was not only as an agent of metallic transformation, but as the very secret of transformation itself, both in the physical and the spiritual realms:

> The Philosopher's Stone is called the most ancient, secret or unknown, natural incomprehensible, heavenly, blessed sacred Stone of the Sages. It is described as being true, more certain than certainty itself, the arcanum of all arcana – the Divine virtue and efficacy, which is hidden from the foolish, the aim and end of all things under heaven, the wonderful epilogue of conclusion of all the labours of the Sages – the perfect essence of all the elements, the indestructible body which no element can injure, the quintessence; the double and living mercury which has in itself the heavenly spirit – the cure for all unsound and imperfect metals – the everlasting light – the panacea for all diseases – the glorious Phoenix – the most precious of all treasures – the chief good of Nature.

> From *The Sophic Hydrolith* (in Waite 1893).

The Stone was seen as the key to knowledge, which only a wise man can use responsibly:

> If an athlete know not the use of his sword, he might as well be without it; and if another warrior that is skilled in the use of that weapon come against him, the first is likely to fare badly. For he that has knowledge and experience on his side, must carry off the victory.

> In the same way, he that possesses this tincture, by the grace of Almighty God, and is unacquainted with its uses, might as well not have it all ... [But] whoever uses this as a medium shall find whither the vestibules of the palace lead, and there is nothing comparable to the subtlety thereof. He shall possess all in all, performing all things whatsoever which are possible under the sun.

> From *The Golden Tripod* (in Waite 1893).

Plainly alchemy was just as much to do with self-mastery as with mastery of the physical laws of Nature, and that neither could be achieved without patience, observation and devotion. Sometimes the aspect of personal transformation was stated very clearly; John of

The Philosopher's Stone, described in terms of sacred geometry, shown here in a form which represents the complete alchemical transformation. (Emblem 21 from Michael Maier's Atlanta Fugiens, *1617.)*

Rupescisia wrote in the fourteenth century that alchemy is 'the secret of the mastery of fixing the sun in our own sky, so that it shines therein and sheds light and the principle of light upon our bodies.'

The alchemical process

The art of the alchemist, then, is to activate a process that will transform a first substance, or *prima materia*, into the Philosopher's Stone. The process is of tremendous importance and carries no guarantee of success, since the attitude of the alchemist, the timing of events, and the type of materials and equipment used, must all harmonise and combine in exactly the right way. Often alchemists spent several decades in their search and attributed their ultimate success to outside aid – either divine or human – rather than to variation in their technique. After looking through various alchemical texts one is left with the impression that there was in fact no one precise formula, which, if followed to the letter, would bring about the desired end. There are only principles of operation that the alchemist must apply with a high level of awareness and judgement. Indeed, the process, with all its potential setbacks and problems, is itself the education of the alchemist, and until he has developed his own skills and insights through this he cannot perfect the Work.

The alchemist is described as the artist who, through his operations, brings Nature to perfection. But the process is also like the unfolding of the Creation of the world, to which the alchemist is a witness as he watches the changes that take place within the vessel. The vessel is a universe in miniature, a crystalline sphere through which he is privileged to see original drama of transformation:

> Neither be anxious to ask whether I actually possess this
> precious treasure. Ask rather whether I have seen how
> the world was created; whether I am acquainted with
> the nature of the Egyptian darkness, what is the cause of
> the rainbow; what will be the appearance of the
> glorified bodies at the general resurrection...

From *The Golden Tripod* (in Waite 1893).

The process itself consists of taking the primal material and subjecting it to chemical treatment, chiefly by heat and distillation, until it finally – perhaps only after years – comes to perfection. The body, soul and spirit of the matter, known as salt, mercury and sulphur, must be freed from their primitive state and reconcile in a new harmony. In terms of physical operation, alchemy differs from chemistry in its insistence on two factors: firstly, the timing of operations to accord with appropriate astrological configurations; and secondly, the repetition of certain stages of the process to an extraordinary extent (such as distilling a liquid several hundred times). Some writers on alchemy, emphasising its value as a spiritual discipline, have belittled the importance of its physical operations, but there is no doubt that the processing of physical substances was equally important in the art. Archibald Cockren, a twentieth-century alchemist, explains the necessity of this:

> That this preparation is a physical process carried out in
> a laboratory with water, retorts, sand-bath, and
> furnaces, there is no doubt. That alchemy is purely a

Astrological charts; horoscopes were used by alchemists to initiate the alchemical process, or to time different stages of the work.
(From sixteenth or seventeenth century English alchemical illustrations, MS Ashmole 1445, section 7: 209. 5, p68, The Bodleian Library, University of Oxford.)

psychic and spiritual science has no basis in fact. A
science to be a science must be capable of
manifestation on every plane of consciousness; in other
words it must be capable of demonstrating the axiom
'as above, so below'. Alchemy can withstand this test,
for it is, physically, spiritually, and psychically, a
science manifesting throughout all form and all life.

(Cockren 1940 (1963: 138))

As I have implied, one can only talk about the different stages of the
process in general terms, since descriptions of it vary. Most texts also
indicate that they are holding back a particular secret, which is
essential for the completion of the operation. Often this relates to the
primal material, the substance needed to start the process, whose
composition is only hinted at. We will look at this fascinating mystery
later, but for the moment it is enough to say that the first material of
alchemy is frequently described as something of metallic origin, yet
not outwardly resembling a metal, a base substance known to all yet
recognised only by the wise. If the substance is treated correctly, it
needs the addition of nothing else to become the Philosopher's Stone,
for it has within its essence the potential power of the stone, and it is
the alchemist's task to bring this potential to realisation:

> For there is only one substance,
> In which all the rest is hidden;
> Therefore, keep good heart.
> Coction, time, and patients are what you need;
> If you would enjoy the precious reward,
> You must cheerfully give both time and labour.
> For you must subject to gentle coction the seeds and the
>   metals,
> Day by day, during several weeks;
> Thus in this one vile thing
> You will discover and bring to perfection the whole
>   work of Philosophy.

From *The Book of Lambspring* (in Waite 1893)

The outward form of the primal material must be destroyed, by fire or
special acidic preparations. Sometimes this is described as setting the
two dragons at war with one another. Thus the male and female
principles of the matter are released and can be reunited in a stage
often depicted as the marriage of the King and Queen. Through initial

An alchemist's laboratory, recreated at Prague Castle, the seat of much alchemical experiment.

conflict and division energy becomes available, a source of fuel for the entire operation. Further treatment of the substance in the vessel by heat leads to its 'death', a moment known as the *nigredo*, or 'blackening'. But the 'soul' of the matter still lingers in the hermetically sealed vessel, and may be induced to condense in liquid form and return to the body once more. This is the resurrection, which may be heralded by a glorious show of iridescent colours known as 'The Peacock's Tail'. The child of the royal union must be gently nurtured, usually by adding a liquid that may have been extracted from the vessel at an earlier stage. With the right food and heat it grows until it 'whitens', indicating that the Elixir is perfected in its first degree. The White Stone, as it is known, is said to be capable of transmuting metals into silver. It is the female tincture, equated with the moon. To gain the gold-giving tincture, the sun, further treatment is necessary until the Elixir reddens. Then it is the Red Rose, grown from the White Rose, the ultimate goal of the process.

As can be seen, alchemy describes its operations in vividly symbolic statements. Terms such as birth, death and resurrection are not used as mere associations but as indications of real states through which the

11

'The Resurrection': the completion of the process and transformation of the base material into alchemical gold. (From MS Ashmole Rolls 53: George Ripley, Alchemical Roll, c. 1600, The Bodleian Library, University of Oxford.)

matter and the soul of the alchemist must pass. The use of beasts, birds and archetypal human figures who fight, marry and copulate expresses the dynamic energies of the process. The different colours of each stage are the heraldic colours of transformation, announcing the dawning of a new 'day' in the creation.

This is the fundamental structure of the alchemical process, but many variants will be discovered, and the order of the stages may differ slightly. The definition of what constitutes a stage in the process is very loose, and authors may claim a different number of essential operations. Usually the number involved is one that is symbolically satisfying, such as seven, ten or twelve – for instance, seven can be likened to the sequence of seven days of creation, the twelve to the number of the zodiacal signs. We shall be looking at individual symbols and stages in more detail later.

Alchemical texts

Alchemical texts are noted for their enigmatic utterances, obscurity and maddening references to unrevealable secrets. Yet they are immensely stimulating, both to the imagination and the intellect, even though there is little consistency of exposition between one text and another, only certain key themes and symbols that recur regularly but not invariably.

One reason for this is that the tradition of alchemy has always been at least half-hidden from public view, and that the texts have been deliberately constructed to conceal certain alchemical directions from the reader. Another reason is that, over the centuries, different schools of alchemy have grown up, each with its own particular code of imagery and philosophical framework. There are obvious differences, for instance, between a Chinese Taoist alchemist and an English Christian alchemist, since the alchemy in question is coloured by the religion and culture of the practitioner. Even within a narrower context it is likely that the different alchemical disciplines were operating: these could probably be defined more closely, but it would be a mammoth task, complicated by the fact that many texts were written anonymously or ascribed to illustrious figures such as Solomon or Isis in order to give them authority.

The reader of alchemical works soon learns to discern the general orientation of alchemical author – whether he was interested in mystical Christian alchemy or in chemical advances, for instance. Readers also need to decide for themselves on the quality and depth of a piece of alchemical writing. Some texts are patently profound, philosophical and lucid, while others are confused, disjointed and superficial. Some plainly speak a measure of truth from a living tradition, whereas others are written from second-hand experience, or else are synthesised in a misguided fashion from other sources. Such an approach may not find favour with scholars, but my view is that anyone interested in the living core of alchemy must find some personal way of penetrating the dense jungle of alchemical books, manuscripts, expositions and illustrations. The alchemical tradition has gathered many great men to it along the way; it has also drawn to it many rogues and fools:

> All that call themselves alchemists are not therefore
> necessarily true possessors of the Stone. For, as in other
> branches of knowledge, there are found many different
> schools and sects, so all that are in search of this
> precious Tincture are called alchemists, without
> necessarily deserving the name.
>
> From *The Sophic Hydrolith* (in Waite 1893).

Chapter Two

The search for transformation

Gold is the focal symbol of alchemy. It is the crowning glory of the Work, the most perfect of metals, and every alchemist has aimed to master the secret of its creation. Gold is more than a metal – it is a principle; and thus, while physical, metallic gold holds a central position in alchemy, yet we also meet with the ideas of exalted gold, vegetable gold, and spiritual gold.

When we look at the properties of gold, it is indisputably a very special metal. It is almost immune to the normal processes of decay and does not rust or tarnish. Fire will refine gold but not destroy it or change its basic nature. Aesthetically it has been described as having 'a smooth, soft texture, a beauty of colour, and a capacity to shine steadily' (Sutherland 1959). For metalworkers, gold has considerable attractions since it can, if necessary, be worked cold. The softness of gold means, that although unsuitable for making sharp or durable implements, delicately tooled shapes and patterns can be crafted, and it can be beaten to an incredible thinness to form gold foil or leaf.

Gold is found in all the continents of the Earth and has been known to every human civilisation. The first known examples of gold worked by man appear around the fourth millennium BC. In Egypt and Ur, gold was used for jewellery, vessels, ornaments, and the adornment of royal tombs. It was not used as currency, however, until about 400 BC. In Egypt gold production was a state-controlled operation and accounts of conditions in the mines paint a gruesome picture of forced labour by criminals and prisoners of war.

From early times, gold was associated with royalty and divinity. The Egyptians called gold 'the flesh of the gods', and, along with other ancient peoples, saw attributes of divinity within gold – effulgence, purity, incorruptibility. Thus gold itself embodied the power of the divine, and could confer especial blessings and gifts through its use. Golden vessels, for instance, were thought to transform the quality of the drink they contained.

Gold also had an early correspondence with the sun, which the alchemists maintained, naming gold and silver as sun and moon, king and queen, the heavenly pair. Gold has also been esteemed universally as a magical, influential, otherworldly metal. In European traditions, fairies and dwarves were thought to be in possession of fabulous amounts of gold, and used it to tempt mortals into their kingdom. It was not merely a symbol of wealth, but an attribution of fairyland itself. There, the roof is made 'o' the beaten gould', the horses are shod with golden shoes, and the music comes from golden harps. Sometimes there is a golden bridge by which the spirits enter and leave their kingdom. Gold is associated with power, danger, enchantment and transformation. In nearly all cultures in which it is esteemed it has been valued as more than a mere metal, and it is this power of gold which the alchemists acknowledged and chose to represent as the goal of their work.

The metalworkers

The craft of metalwork helped to build a foundation for alchemy, and had already been in existence long before alchemy itself first came to light around 200 BC. Alchemy was strongly influenced by Egyptian traditions, and Egypt had been a centre for metal workers who raised their craft to a high degree. They knew how to make alloys, and how to tint metals; they could colour gold with varnishes and understood gold-plating. Some of their art was directed towards satisfying the ever-present human desire to obtain more for less, since there were recipes for debasing gold with other metals to increase its apparent weight, and even to make fake gold.

However, the craftsmen undoubtedly took a great pride in their work, and they guarded its secrets jealously. We have few details of how it was practised, but certain general principles are known from paintings or hieroglyphs of the time. The smelter's furnace, for instance, was built up high on three sides to intensify the heat when the metal was being refined, and a blowpipe was used to increase the heat of the flames. The earliest alchemists would probably have been initiated into the art of metalwork, but exactly how and when the two arts began to take on a separate identity is not certain.

The first alchemists in the West

We only know of the existence of alchemists if they chose to reveal their presence, and if their writings have survived them. Therefore, while the earliest alchemical texts we now have date from the third century BC, according to some authorities, we cannot tell how many practising alchemists there were before this date, or how strong the tradition was at its recorded inception, since there are very few texts available until we come to the fourth to seventh centuries AD, the period that marks the first flowering of alchemy in the West. Although the alchemists themselves have always claimed a venerable pedigree for their art, stretching back to Plato, Moses and the god Hermes himself, this is no help in dating its origins.

These claims sprang from a philosophy which maintained that in the past man was the master of all wisdom, and that his passage through time has been marked by a gradual forgetting of the ancient secrets which only true initiates had kept uncorrupted throughout the centuries. It was common, therefore for authors to establish a worthy pedigree for their writings, by ascribing their teachings to earlier masters, or by claiming direct descent from the original divine or mythical patrons of the art. It was an attempt to lend weight to their words, rather than to deceive. Nevertheless, this does not help the historian, and we find that the beginnings of alchemy are shrouded in obscurity. The first known and named alchemical text is probably that by **Bolos of Mendes,** who wrote a book entitled *Physika*. This dealt with a variety of alchemical and pseudo-alchemical crafts, such as the making of gold, silver, gems, and the production of purple dye. Bolos tried to ascribe his work to the philosopher Demokrites (Democritus), father of the atomic theory, who lived in the fifth century BC. Possibly the writings of Bolos date to around 250 BC, but some authorities would regard them as products of the first or second century AD. Other early extant texts are known as the Leiden and Stockholm Papyri, but these, while going under the name of alchemy, seem to be merely collections of recipes for making false gold and silver and for tinting and alloying metals. One recipe begins: 'To give objects of copper the appearance of gold so that neither the feel nor rubbing on the touchstone will discover it... '

With these texts we move to the early years of the current era, and to the flourishing Alexandrian culture in which alchemy throve. Alexandria was founded as a city by the Emperor Alexander on the north coast of Egypt in the fourth century BC and soon became a centre of great influence in the fields of philosophy, mathematics, astrology, science, medicine, and indeed every other branch of learning then practised. It was a city of mixed nationalities, containing Greek, Jewish, Egyptian, Persian, Syrian and Christian inhabitants. When powerful cultures meet in peace or war there is often a remarkable stimulation of ideas; the coming together of the European and Arabic cultures at the time of the Crusades can be cited as an example. In Alexandria this contact was affirmed and crystallized through the founding of schools of learning and the establishment of the great Alexandrian library. Scholars travelled from far and wide to study the ancient and contemporary texts housed there, which represented the whole spectrum of knowledge of the classical and Egyptian civilizations. Had this library not been destroyed at a later date by the Arab invasion, our knowledge of the ancient world would be infinitely greater than it is.

Another notable name from this early period of Alexandrian alchemy is that of **Maria the Jewess,** who is quoted with respect by other alchemists of the time and who lived around AD 100. She seems to have been a practical and inventive lady who improved the alchemical apparatus of the day. The *bain-marie* is named after her – the warm water bath that allows gentle cooking and that is still used in modern kitchens. Certain other texts from the same period are ascribed to **Kleopatra,** and while most historians are inclined to regard this as an attempt to elevate the famous Queen Cleopatra to the status of an alchemical priestess, Jack Lindsay, on the other hand, considers that the works originate from the school of a different Kleopatra, a lady alchemist of the time whose teachings were perpetuated by her disciples. The writings in question are *The Dialogue of Kleopatra and the Philosophers* and *The Gold-Making of Kleopatra*. From the former comes a precise description of the alchemical process:

> Take from the four elements the arsenic which is highest
> and lowest, the white and the red, the male and the
> female in equal balance, so that they may be joined to
> one another. For just as the bird warms her eggs with
> her heat and brings them to their appointed term, so
> yourselves warm your composition and bring it to its
> appointed term. And when you've borne it out and
> caused it to drink of the divine Waters in the Sun and in
> heated places, cook it upon a gentle fire with the

virginal milk, keeping it from the smoke. Then shut the
ingredients up in Hades and stir carefully until the
preparation becomes thicker and does not run from the
fire. Then remove it from the fire; and when the soul
and spirit are unified and become one, project upon the
body of silver and you will have gold such as the
treasuries of kings do not contain.

(Lindsay 1970:256)

One of the best known authors of the period is **Zosimos,** whose
writings give us some fine examples of visionary alchemy which will
be considered in the next chapter.

Laboratory work was certainly prominent in early alchemy, and a good
deal of information survives as to the type of equipment used.
Cupellation, a technique already known in ancient Egypt, was used to
refine metals. A cupel consisted of a crucible, made usually of bone
ash, which was supported by its lips about the edge of a furnace. The
metal to be refined was placed within it and it was subjected to intense
heat, sometimes closed in a kiln for several days until the impurities
were either driven off by the heat or absorbed into the crucible itself.

A special feature of alchemy was distillation, and it remained a
technique unique to alchemy for many centuries (see page 129). A
still, or alembic was used. The material to be heated would be placed
at the bottom of the still; there was a cool section above to condense
the vapour driven off by the heat, and some means of collecting the
liquid thus distilled.

Maria the Jewess, mentioned above for her prowess in designing more
efficient apparatus, invented a new still which Zosimos describes:

Make three cubes of ductile copper a little thicker than
that of a pastry cooks copper frying pan: their length
should be about a cubit and a half. Make three such
tubes and also make a wide tube of a hand's breadth
width and an opening proportioned to that of the still
head. The three tubes should have their openings
adapted like a nail to the neck of a light receiver, so that
they have that the thumb tube and the two finger-tubes
joined laterally on either hand. Towards the bottom of
the still-head are three holes adjusted to the tubes, and
when these are fitted they are soldered in place, the one
above receiving the vapour in a different fashion. Then

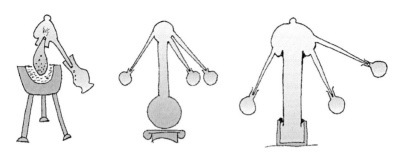

Different types of stills used in alchemical apparatus over the centuries.

> setting the still-head upon the earthenware pan
> containing the sulphur, and luting the joints with flour
> paste, place at the ends of the tubes glass flasks, large
> and strong so that they may not break with the heat
> coming from the water in the middle.

(Lindsay 1970: 245)

For a discussion of what this still and other alchemical apparatus of the early period looked like see Sherwood Taylor, *The Alchemists*, (Taylor 1976 Ch. 4).

Although sulphur is mentioned here as the material to be distilled, quite possibly this did not refer to sulphur as we know it but to Primal Material, the secret substance that is transformed into the gold-making tincture. Sulphur, mercury and salt in alchemical terminology refer to the three qualities of matter – spirit, soul and body respectively – and not to the common substances of these names. Sometimes one of these terms would be used to designate the first material of the operation.

Another invention of the time was the *kerotakis*, a piece of equipment that created vapours out of a substance, through the application of heat; the vapours would then affect a portion of metal placed in the top part of the apparatus. The result would frequently emerge as an alloy, but it is likely that the idea of imparting colour through the use of the *kerotakis* was also important, since the word carries the meaning of 'artist's palette'.

From the earliest days, colour changes have played a significant part in alchemy. Each stage of the process has been associated with a different colour, and a correct sequence of colour changes has always been considered of critical importance in ascertaining whether the work is

19

proceeding along the right lines. To the alchemists, colour has always been much more than an outward quality of matter; colour is the *pneuma* or life spirit of a substance. Changes of colour are a visible sign that transformation is taking place within matter.

The Greek alchemists recognised four distinct stages of colour change in the process, a successive blackening, whitening, yellowing and reddening of the material in the vessel. (Sometimes red and purple were used synonymously.) Black was equated with the death of matter, and white with its rebirth in a purified form. The exact meaning of the yellowing is not clear, and this stage was often omitted in later descriptions of alchemy; but the reddening was always seen as the final perfection of the matter that had been transformed from a gross state into the longed-for Stone or Tincture. Although it was considered that no stage had been successfully accomplished unless the appropriate colour was manifested, yet it should be noted that colour on its own did not necessarily denote success. Warning is given, for instance, of a premature reddening, which could occur through hasty and careless work and which must be corrected at once.

The key sequence of black, white and red has remained throughout the history of alchemy, with occasional variations and additions. The most common addition is that of the iridescent stage known as the Peacock's Tail, the rainbow, or the starry sky, which usually occurs after the *nigredo*, or blackening. Colour is an intrinsic part of the alchemical drama; with a little imagination the reader can easily see how, after perhaps months of patient observation, the alchemist was affected profoundly by the appearance of a new and dazzling hue in the hermetic vessel.

Theories of elements and metals

> There are four elements, and... each has at its centre
> another element which makes it what it is. These are the
> four pillars of the world. They were in the beginning
> evolved and moulded out of chaos by the hand of the
> Creator; and it is their contrary action which keeps up
> the harmony and equilibrium of the mundane
> machinery; it is they, which through the virtue of
> celestial influences, produce all things above and
> beneath the earth.

> From Sendivogius *The New Chemical Light* (in Waite
> 1893).

Here a black dragon represents the nigredo, *a dramatic stage of alchemy when all hope seems to be lost. Figure 2 from* The Book of Lambspring *(in Waite 1893).*

Michael Sendivogius, writing in the seventeenth century, is here describing a classical theory of the construction of matter that formed the basis of ideas on alchemical transformation from the early period until the eighteenth century. The four elements are earth, water, fire and air, and were first mentioned by the Greek philosopher Empedocles, who flourished *circa* 450 BC. These were seen as combining in different proportions to form every substance in existence; in alchemy part of the task was to rearrange the composition of the elements and their relationship to one another in order to transform the substance itself.

Aristotle's exposition of the theory was formulated *circa* 350 BC and held sway in Europe until the new era of science dawned in the seventeenth century. He held that each element was composed of two qualities, there being four qualities in all – hot, dry, moist and cold. The element of air was hot and moist; fire was hot and dry; earth dry and cold; and water cold and moist. By changing a quality of each element, transformation became possible: by driving out the moisture from air, for instance, fire would result since the pair of qualities would now be those of fire, which was hot and dry. This provided the alchemists with a theory of transformation.

The apparent simplicity of this system, however, is undermined by the alchemists' own descriptions of it, as we can see from the quotation above. They were quick to point out that true air, fire, water and earth were not the common entities that we know. The 'common' elements were the visible or tangible qualities that came closest in character to the 'pure' elements. These pure elements were found only at the very heart of matter, and were seen more as forces, or agencies, rather than as detectable substances. They carried out the work of Nature by combining and recombining to create all the different types of matter on the earth. If matter changed its state, as it did in the alchemical vessel, then this signified that the proportions of elements forming the matter had been transformed and recombined. A change in the elemental state could not be brought about by mere physical force, such as by grinding or cutting. Usually it was thought to be produced only by the application of another elemental agent, that of fire or water especially.

Thus 'common' fire and water played a prominent part in alchemy, but frequently the alchemists sought to make the 'pure' forms, which they called by such names as 'our fire' and 'the sweet water', the 'Pontic water' or 'the water of the wise'. These were the subject of lengthy preparation and were used for such purposes as the destruction of the original form of the Primal Material in order to liberate the elements within it, or for nourishing the material in the vessel when it had already undergone radical transformation.

Gold was considered to contain the perfect balance of all four elements. Nature, it was said, operated a constant process of perfecting that which was originally gross or corrupt. Aristotle, once again, was responsible for first putting forward the theory that Nature 'grew' gold in the earth and that all metals, in due course, would grow to become

*The four elements, earth, water, fire and air, shown as four sisters,
within the complex system of correspondences in alchemy.
(From Johann Daniel Mylius,* Philosophia Reformata, *1622)*

gold. Metals themselves grew from seeds, which might not normally be
recognised as being metallic in their primal state. Sometimes the
alchemical quest for the Primal Material was described as a search for
the right metallic seed, which the alchemist could nurture and grow
into its perfect golden state. Aristotle suggested that metals were
produced within the earth by the action of vapour. Alchemists
elaborated this idea, inferring that the warmth of the sun and the
influence of the planets activate this vapour, and that because these
factors vary according to the climate, the seasons, and the planetary
configurations, so the types of metals laid down in the earth will vary.
In the alchemical process they sought to imitate this, by taking the
degree of heat in the furnace, the time of year, and the astrological
indications into account. By observing Nature, the wise handmaid of
the Divine Will, the alchemist could begin to understand her ways, it
was said, and learn how to imitate and improve on them through Art.

The alchemist's view of the earth was of a living organism that was in a constant state of change and growth. In alchemy there is no such thing as 'dead' matter; all substance has life and movement.

Eastern alchemy: the search for the elixir

In many ways the development of alchemy in the Far East is remarkably similar to that of alchemy in the West, especially in the first thousand years of their existence. Scholars are not able to agree about the reasons for this. Some argue that alchemy began in the East and was transmitted by connections as yet untraced to the West, while some consider the reverse to be more likely. Others, such as H.J. Shepperd argue for independent origins in East and West, with possible cross-fertilization at a later stage, such as a Chinese influence on Arabian alchemy in the seventh century AD. Shepperd points out that metallurgic skills developed independently in different cultures as a natural part of human evolution, and that these involved a secrecy and mystery that would have given rise to alchemical work almost spontaneously (Shepperd 1970).

There are differences of emphasis in the Eastern and Western histories of alchemy, even though both sought the transformation of earthly materials into a divine potency. In the West the quest was primarily concerned with the transmutation of gold, whether for physical or spiritual purposes. In the East alchemists aspired to make a perfect elixir of gold which would bring immortality to the soul and supernatural powers to the mind, such as the ability to tap the knowledge of the celestial beings:

> My teacher also used to say that if one wished for perpetual life one should diligently take the great medicines, and that if one desired to communicate with the gods and spirits one should use solutions of metals and practise the multiplication of one's person. By multiplying the person one will be able automatically to see the three *hun* souls and the seven *pho* souls within one's body. One will also be able to enter the presence of the powers and principalities of the heavens, and the deities of the earth, as well as having the spirits of all the mountains and rivers in one's service.
>
> (Ko Hung [*circa* AD 300] quoted in Needham 1956)

Gold was venerated in the East from ancient times. One of the Indian Vedas, written around the eighth century BC, mentions the use of a golden talisman to prolong life, and from the seventh century BC comes the saying: 'Gold is indeed fire, light and immortality'. The first real records of alchemy date from the first few centuries AD, paralleling Western development. Although we know that alchemy was practised in India, Tibet and Burma, the best information available to us concerns China, mainly because of the researches of Joseph Needham.

Alchemy in China had its roots in Taoism, a branch of religious philosophy. In both alchemy and Taoism there seems to be an idea of a Spirit in all things that is greater than anything else in the world, and yet ignored by all:

> The great Tao flows everywhere, both to the left and to
>   the right.
> The ten thousand things depend upon it; it holds
>   nothing back.
> It fulfils its purpose silently and makes no claim.
> It nourishes the ten thousand things, And yet is not their
>   lord. It has no aim; it is very small.
> The ten thousand things return to it, Yet it is not their
>   lord. It is very great.
> It does not show greatness, And is therefore truly great.

> (*Tao Te Ching*; translated J. Needham)

(Compare this with the description of the first material on page 49.)

Alchemy in China absorbed other elements of the prevailing culture and philosophies. The school of the Naturalists (*circa* 350–270 BC) promoted an interest in science and the discovery of the properties of matter. Five elements were said to compose the basis of the material world: they were called earth, wood, metal, fire and water. These did not have quite the same connotations as the classical Western elements, and appear to have defined qualities of plasticity and permeability. The element of wood, for instance, was said to represent that quality in matter which determines whether a surface is curved or straight; the element of metal was taken as the property of a substance that allows melting and moulding to take place.

Alchemy in the West used astrology as a guide to the correct timing of events; Chinese alchemy did the same, and added the use of the

I Ching, the divinatory *Book of Changes.* Chinese alchemy did not restrict itself solely to the preparation of the Elixir, but also embodied a quest for transmutation of metals as a subsidiary interest. Huan T'an, in the first century BC, was said to have a drug that would convert quicksilver into gold. Neither were charlatans restricted to Western alchemy, as we may infer their existence in China from an edict published around 144 BC commanding public execution of all those who were counterfeiting gold.

Laboratory experiment was an intrinsic part of Eastern alchemical practice. This led to the understanding of various chemical principles and by about the third century BC the Taoists had already grasped the technique of condensation. In the fourth century AD an emperor set up a Taoist laboratory to conduct alchemical experiments. This particular establishment had a rather curious aspect to it, however; condemned criminals were used as guinea pigs to test the elixirs that the industrious alchemists produced! One wonders whether this was a cruel and cowardly procedure, or a generous gesture to give the condemned men one last chance!

Chapter Three
Dreams and revelations

How did alchemists acquire their knowledge? There were teachers, manuscripts and, later, printed books from which they might learn. But accounts of alchemical discoveries frequently relate that the key to the mystery was found through a personal vision or revelation. It was also emphasised that such illumination could only come to those who were sincere, persistent, and well-prepared to receive the secret knowledge:

> A most wonderful Magistery and Archimagistery is the Tincture of sacred Alchemy, the marvellous science of the secret Philosophy, the singular gift bestowed upon men through the grace of Almighty God – which men have never discovered through the labour of their own hands, but only by revelation and the teaching of others.

(Norton 1477)

This idea of a direct revelation, frequently expressed through a vision or dream, clarifies many of the aspects of alchemy which at first seem bewildering. It sheds light on why alchemical descriptions are nearly always given in terms of verbal or pictorial symbols, and helps us to understand why no one account of the alchemical process ever seems to follow exactly the same lines as another. Even allowing for the difference between individual schools of alchemy, the fact is that each alchemist demonstrates his art in an original way, just as no person's dream is ever exactly the same as another's.

The philosophy underlying this approach to alchemy, but by no means unique to it, is that knowledge exists, and that we can attune ourselves to receive it. According to this concept, individual consciousness can link into consciousness of a higher order and learn from it. Knowledge revealed in this way is unlikely to surface in a precise or literal form; it exists in the realm of what we call 'archetypes', a level of life at which the principles of creation are present, rather than as particular, individual manifestations of it. It will be received more as the seed of an idea, something that can be developed, and given an external application. Moreover, a person will receive and understand an idea according to his own cultural background and the age in which he lives. Knowledge is like a pool; a man dips his pitcher into the pool and the water he carries away adapts itself to the form of this particular container. The idea that we, as human beings, have an opportunity to acquire knowledge this way is reflected in the early Hermetic writings, dating from around the third century A.D., and purporting to be the words of the sage Hermes Trismegistus. (See discussion of the Emerald Tablet in Chapter Four) In the following passage, mind is equated with *gnosis*, or knowledge:

> It was [God's] will... that mind should be placed in the midst as a prize that human souls may win... He filled a great basin with mind and sent it down to earth; and he appointed a herald, and bade him make a proclamation to the hearts of men: 'Hearken, each human heart; dip yourself in this basin, if you can, recognizing for what purpose you have been made, and believing that you shall ascend to Him who sent the basin down.' Now those who gave heed to the proclamation, and dipped themselves in the bath of mind, these men got a share of *gnosis*; they received mind and so became complete men.

> (Scott 1924 [1985: 151])

Alchemy is not alone in transmitting a tradition of personal revelation as a means of penetrating the mysteries of the world. Many religions embody accounts of dreams, visions and encounters with divine messengers that bring wisdom and understanding, and it is generally accepted that the most profound religious understanding is likely to come through its revelation and internal illumination. Less common, perhaps, is the idea that knowledge can also arise in this way, through personal revelation. We have become used to the idea that 'facts' and 'theories' are built up only through a process of trial and error and planned experiment. Yet, it seems, this is far from the truth, even in science, as A.M. Taylor was one of the first to point out: 'The history of science shows us, again and again, great discoveries made by passionate adherence to ideas forged in the white heat of imagination.' (Taylor 1966) He also reminds us that some of the most important scientific ideas did not fit the facts as they could be demonstrated, and

A monk-alchemist receiving the secrets of the Great Work through a vision imparted by an angel. (From MS Ashmole Rolls 53: George Ripley, Alchemical Roll, circa 1600, The Bodleian Library, University of Oxford.)

that the scientists concerned had to persist with their visions, despite the apparent evidence, until the data available could expand to demonstrate the truth of their theories.

Over thirty years later scientists may be shy of admitting the power of the Idea, and even more wary of ascribing its birth to the activity of a higher form of consciousness, but alchemy had no such scruples and indeed the alchemists believed that their art could never be mechanical and would only be accomplished through access to a source of wisdom. (Even those who were taught by a living adept held, by and large, to the idea that 'the master will come when the pupil is ready'.) The chief medium of alchemical revelation, the way in which the 'Idea' surfaced into consciousness, was that of the vision. The *Corpus Hermeticum*, a body of hermetic writings originating from the early centuries of the Christian era (see page 116) begins thus:

> Once upon a time, when I had begun to think about the
> things that are, and my thoughts had soared high aloft,
> while my bodily senses had been put under restraint by
> sleep – yet not such sleep as that of men weighed down
> by fullness of food or by bodily weariness – me thought
> there came to me a Being of vast and boundless

magnitude, who called me by name, and said to me, 'What do you wish to hear and see, and to learn and to come to know by thought?' 'Who are you?' I said. 'I,' said he, 'am Poimandres, the Mind of the Sovereignty. 'I would feign learn,' said I, 'the things that are, and understand their nature, and get knowledge of God.'

The dreamer is then taught about the role of the elements of nature in the creation of the world.

One of the most famous visionary alchemical accounts was written by Zosimos and included in his work *On Virtue* (fourth century AD). He recounts that he fell asleep while reciting alchemical formulae to himself and:

I saw a sacrificing priest who stood above me by an altar shaped like a chalice. The altar had fifteen steps leading up to it. The priest stood up, and I heard a loud voice from above which said to me, 'I have completed the act of descending the fifteen steps, walking into darkness, and the act of climbing the steps towards the light. It is the sacrifices who renews me by rejecting the denseness of the body. Thus, consecrated a priest by necessity, I become a spirit.

Having heard the voice of him who stood above on the chalice-shaped altar, I demanded to know who he was. And he, in a shrill voice replied thus: 'I am Ion, the priest of the sanctuaries, and I have undergone intolerable violence. Someone came suddenly in the morning and he took me by force, cleaving me in two with a sword, dismembering me, following the rules of combination. He took off all the skin from my head with the sword which he held, he mixed my bones with my flesh, and he burnt them in the fire of the process. It was thus that I learnt, through the transformation of the body, to become a spirit, so intolerable was the violence.' As I forced him to speak to me thus, his eyes became like blood and he vomited up all his flesh. And I saw him take the appearance of a tiny man, tearing himself with his own teeth and falling away.

Filled with fear, I woke up and I thought, 'Is this not the composition of the waters?' I told myself that I had understood this well, and I fell asleep again.

More visions follow, which Zosimos interprets as being teachings about the divine water, giving him a complete key to the process of alchemical transformation.

> In a word, when all things are brought to agreement by division and union, without neglecting the process, nature is transformed; for nature, returning to herself, transforms herself, and this concerns the quality and the bond of virtue throughout the whole universe.

Zosimos then turns his whole vision into a symbolic description of the alchemical process to serve as a model for other seekers:

> In brief, my friend, build a temple of one stone, resembling white lead, alabaster, with no beginning nor end in its construction. It should have within it a source of pure water, sparkling like the sun. Observe carefully on which side of the temple the entrance lies, and, taking a sword in your hand, seek out the entrance, for the opening is narrow indeed. A serpent sleeps at the entrance, guarding the temple. Seize him, and sacrifice him; skin him, and, taking his flesh and bones, dismember him. Then reunite his parts with his bones at the entrance to the temple, and, making a step of him, climb up and enter; you will find there that which you seek. The priest, this man of copper, whom you will see seated in the spring, mustering his colour, should not be thought of as a man of copper, for he has changed the colour of his nature and become a man of silver. If you wish, you will soon have him as a man of gold.

> (Cornelius Agrippa, *Of Occult Philosophy, 1655*; translated by author.)

The vision described has far more power than that of a mere chemical experiment put into colourful terms. For alchemists, what is true on a physical, or chemical level, is also true at the emotional and spiritual level, and their goal is to achieve transformation on all three levels at once. Thus it becomes clear why the language of dreams and visions is such an appropriate medium for alchemy, for the symbols can contain these different levels of meaning simultaneously.

Another well-known alchemical vision is that of George Ripley, who lived in the fifteenth century. In *The Vision* he wrote:

When busie at my Book I was upon a certain Night,
> This Vision here exprest appear'd unto my dimmed
> sight:

A Toad full Ruddy I saw, did drink the juice of Grapes
> so fast,

Till over-charged with the broth, his Bowels all to brast:
> And after that, from poyson'd Bulk he cast his
> Venom fell,

For Grief and Pain whereof his Members all began to
> swell;

With drops of poysoned sweat approaching thus his
> secret Den,

His Cave with blasts of fumous Air he all bewhited then:

And from the which in space a Golden Humour did
> ensue,

Whose falling drops from high did stain the soyl with
> ruddy hue.

And when his Corps the force of vital breath began to
> lack,

This dying Toad became forthwith like Coal for colour
> Black:

Thus drowned in his proper veins of poysoned flood;
> For term of Eighty days and Four he rotting stood By
> Tryal then this Venom to expel I did desire; For
> which I did commit his Carkass to a gentle Fire:
> Which done, a Wonder to the sight, but more to be
> rehearst;

The Toad with Colours rare through every side was
> pierc'd,

And White appear'd when all the sundry hews were
> past:

Which after being tincted Ruddy, for evermore did last.
> Then of the Venom handled thus a Medicine I did
> make; Which Venom kills, and saveth such as
> Venom chance to take:

Glory be to him the granter of such secret ways,
> Dominion, and Honour both, with Worship, and
> with Praise.

Amen

(Ashmole1652: 375)

'Contrition of Matter': a toad represents the Primal Material, the basis of the alchemical work, and from which the serpent energy is released to be transformed into gold. (Hand-coloured engraving from MS of Elias Ashmole, Theatrum Chemicum Britannicum, *seventeenth century, opp. p.28, The Bodleian Library, University of Oxford.)*

The alchemical process is unfolded through this sequence. The first matter, the Toad (an image which is in accordance with the idea that the primal material may be despised and rejected by men because of its outer appearance), is fed with alchemical water until it bursts (separates) and releases its spirit while the body putrefies (the *nigredo*). Then it is reheated and the 'Peacock's Tail' stage of many colours occurs, being followed by whitening and then reddening, which is the formation of the Tincture, or Stone.

Perhaps it may seem too neat that a fully-fledged symbolic account of the alchemical process should arise in George Ripley's head as he pored over his books. It may indeed be true that the alchemist artistically shaped his or her dreams to present a more coherent picture of their intrinsic meaning, especially in a literary context. However, such dreams and visions were states for which these practitioners actively strove, and we know now that, asleep or awake, it is possible to have some measure of control over the progress of a dream, both in inducing it and in influencing its direction. 'Lucid dreaming' has been rediscovered and recognised by psychologists of today, although the faculty has existed since time immemorial and been practised in various traditions and cultures. While asleep, the subject may be aware that he or she is dreaming, and can make active choices about its development. This can give access to a more powerful level of imagery, and may also create more of a 'story' within the dream, engendered by a combination of spontaneous imagination, awareness, and active intention. A guide figure is a common feature of such dreams, and the dreamer may be encouraged to question and to follow the guide for the purpose of gaining deeper knowledge. The main difference between the alchemical and the psychological outlook is that the psychologist would see dream content as giving insight into patterns and events in the dreamer's own life, whereas the alchemist perceives the flow of imagery as emblems of occult truth, the secrets of creation explained in symbolic form.

Additionally, dreams may be encouraged to unfold while one is awake. Again, this technique has been known for centuries but is only now re-emerging into general awareness; it is often called 'guided imagery' or 'visualisation'. The imaginative faculty is allowed to work as internal vision, either moving freely or else focusing on a set theme, such as following a pathway, visiting a garden, entering a castle, and so on. A certain level of awareness must persist, or else images disintegrate into fragmented daydreams; this is why the exercise is often carried out in groups, or with a trained leader. Images that arise this way often have much of the stirring quality of dream imagery, but without its confusion.

Alchemists probably took the pursuit of vision to this active stage. We can note that Ripley described his sight as 'dimmed' but did not say that he was sleeping. Even more telling are the words of John Dastin, whose alchemical poem, *Dastin's Dream*, begins:

> Not yet full sleeping, nor yet full waking,
> But between the twain lying in a trance;
> Halfe closed mine Eyes in my slumbering...
> Towards Aurora, ere Phoebus uprise,
> I dreamed one came to me to do me pleasaunce
> That brought me a book with seven seals close ...
> Following upon I had a wonderful dream,
> As seemed to my inward thought,
> The face of him shone as the sun beam:
> Which unto me this heavenly book brought,
> Of so great riches that it may not be bought.

The visions of the alchemists, it would seem, might occur in sleep, semi-consciousness or the waking state, sometimes triggered by long hours spent poring over books or prolonged periods of concentration

as they watched the alchemical vessels for signs of change. Some may
have come unbidden, as welcome but unexpected revelations which
brought the insight that was needed; others may have been induced
deliberately.

Cornelius Agrippa, magician, philosopher and alchemist of the
sixteenth century, described how men may prepare themselves to
receive significant dreams:

> Now I call that a dream, which proceedeth either from
> the spirit of the phantasie and intellect united together,
> or by the illustration of the Agent intellect above our
> souls, or by the true revelation of some divine power in
> a quiet and purified mind; for by this our soul receiveth
> true oracles, and abundantly yieldeth prophecies to us:
> for in dreams we seem both to ask questions, and learn
> to read and find them out... It is necessary, that he who
> should receive true dreams, should keep a pure,
> undisturbed, and an undisquieted imaginative spirit, and
> so compose it, that it may be made worthy of the
> knowledge and government by the mind and
> understanding... When therefore we are found in body,
> not disturbed in mind, not dulled by meat or drink, nor
> sad through poverty, nor provoked by any advice or lust
> or wrath, but chastely going to bed, fall asleep, then our
> pure and divine soul being loosed from all hurtful
> thoughts, and now freed by dreaming, is endowed with
> this divine spirit as an instrument, and doth receive
> those beams and representations, which are darted
> down, and shine forth from the divine mind into itself;
> and as it were in a deifying glass, it does far more
> certainly, clearly, and efficaciously behold all things,
> then by the vulgar inquiry of the intellect, and by the
> discourse of reason...

To whom or to what did the alchemists ascribe their visions? They
knew that what they saw and experienced came from a greater source
of power than that of their own imaginations. Many gladly gave thanks
to God for the illumination they had received. But many also
perceived a guide or spirit who acted as a medium for the vision. The
author of the Hermetic text obtained his knowledge from Poimandres,
'the Mind of the Sovereignty', who was perceived as a great being.
Another work, dating from the Arabic period of alchemy, but possibly

having earlier origins, is entitled *The Book of Thirty Chapters*, and here the vision is granted by an unnamed being, possibly Hermes Trismegistus (the 'patron saint' of alchemy):

> When I realized that love of the Great Work had fallen into my heart and that the preoccupations I felt about it had chased sleep from my eyes, that they prevented me from eating and drinking so that my body was wasting away and my appearance was bad, I gave myself up to prayer and fasting. I begged God to drive out the miseries and cares that had taken hold of my heart, and put an end to the perplexed situation in which I found myself.

> While I lay asleep on my couch, a being appeared to me in a dream and told me, 'Rise up and understand what I am going to show you.'

> I rose up and went off with this person. Soon we arrived before Seven Gates so fine that I had never seen the like. 'Here,' my guide said to me, 'are found the treasures of the science you seek.'

> 'Thank you,' I replied. 'Now guide me so that I may penetrate into these dwellings where you say are found the treasures of the universe.'

> 'You will never penetrate there,' he answered, 'unless you have in your power the keys of those doors. But come with me. I'll show you the keys of those doors.'

Each door corresponds to a metal associated with a planet and the aspirant is given teaching at each one. (The notion of seven gates to be passed through is strongly reminiscent of the Mithraic tradition, where initiates had to pass through seven realms ruled by planets in order to return to the source of all creation.) He is taught the relationship between body, soul and spirit, and between the elements, and is instructed in many other aspects of alchemy through word and emblem. Finally, another guide, an old man, shows him a three-bodied animal, the 'Key of Science', whose parts devour one another.

> The old man said to me, 'Man, go and find that animal, give him an intelligence in place of yours, a vital spirit in place of yours, a life in place of yours; then he'll submit to you and give you all you need.'

A depiction of Hermes
Trismegistus on the
pavement of Siena
Cathedral, Italy, a figure
representing wisdom and
vision.

> As I wondered how I could give anyone an intelligence
> in place of mine, a vital spirit in place of mine, an
> existence in place of mine, the old man said, 'Take the
> body that is like your own, take from it what I have just
> told you, and hand it over to him.'
>
> I did as the old man bade me, and I acquired then the
> whole science, as complete as that described by
> Hermes.
>
> (Quoted in Lindsay 1970: 147)

Zosimos formulated a philosophy of revelation, suggesting that there
was a universal being of man, with body, soul and spirit, and that it is
this 'Great Man' who comes in various guises to teach the individual:

> In effect the Nous, our god, declares:
>
> 'The Son of God, who can do all things and become all
> things as he wishes, shows himself as he wishes to each
> man.
>
> And up to this day, and on till the end of the world, in
> secret and in hidden ways, he comes to those who are
> his and communicates with them, counselling them, in
> secret and by means of their intellect, to separate
> themselves from their Adam,* who blinds them and
> who grudges the spiritual and luminous man.'
>
> (* Adam is the base and ignorant aspect of man.)

37

Nicholas Flamel, a fourteenth-century alchemist saw his guiding light as an angel, who appeared to him while he was in a deep sleep, showing him an ancient, handsome volume, and telling him that he would one day understand its contents. Later he found this very book on sale and discovered it to be an old alchemical manuscript.

One of the most curious alchemical stories in which the aspirant seeks guidance comes from the pen of Bolos, a Greek alchemist. He tells us that his teacher Ostanes died before his instruction was completed. Bolos decided to summon up the spirit of his worthy master, and succeeding in this, he demanded further alchemical information from him. Ostanes remained silent during this badgering, and only when addressed more respectfully did he choose to speak, telling Bolos, 'The books are in the temple.' Bolos and his fellow students searched the temple thoroughly but found nothing. Some time later, they were enjoying a banquet in the temple when suddenly one of the columns split open. They rushed to see if the sacred tomes were hidden inside, but found only one simple formula inscribed there: 'A nature is delighted by another nature, a nature conquers another nature, a nature dominates another nature.' This, said Bolos, gave them the key to the alchemical art; the saying was also held in great reverence by later alchemists..

The alchemical accounts clearly show that the Great Work was seen as having a divine origin, and that teaching must be obtained either through a great sage, whether living or dead, or through a direct vision that would serve as a basis for the work. Little wonder, then, that we find gods, goddesses, Biblical and mythical sages all claimed as founders of the art. Perhaps the boldest claim is that God gave 'the medicine' to Adam, and that it was passed from him to the chosen few who have perpetuated a line of succession. In the early days of alchemy, it was often implied that the perfect knowledge of alchemy could be found hidden in one very special book, or inscribed on a column in a certain temple. Sometimes the all-important text was thought to be hidden in the tomb of a king. Alchemists from the fifteenth to the seventeenth century in Europe dwelt on the same theme, but usually expressed it in terms of the constant search by the student for the one right book among the hundreds of fraudulent and mendacious texts available. This is the myth of the perfect knowledge, described as once known and then nearly lost, lingering still in an obscure, secret or hidden place. But the knowledge is never found except through the Divine Will:

Angels guide the spirit of
the alchemist into new
realms of discovery, here
mirrored in the Biblical
story of Jacob's dream of
the ladder stretching
between heaven and
earth. (From Mutus Liber,
1677.)

Our Art, its theory as well as its practice, is altogether a
gift of God, Who gives it when and to whom He elects
... Though I had diligently studied this Art for seventeen
or eighteen years, yet I had, after all, to wait for God's
own time, and accept it as a free gift. No one need
doubt the truth or certainty of this Art. It is as true and
certain, and as surely ordained by God in nature, as it is
that the sun shines at noon-tide, and the moon shews
forth her soft splendour at night.

From *The Golden Tract* (in Waite 1893)

In the later centuries of alchemy, especially in the sixteenth and
seventeenth centuries, there seem to be fewer accounts of direct
visions, perhaps because alchemical authors of this period were keen
to introduce more philosophical discourse into their works. But the
visionary quality lived on, and was often deliberately introduced in the
form of parables or allegories, as in the lengthy *Chymical Wedding of
Christian Rosenkreutz* (see page 59). Or in *A Subtle Allegory
Concerning the Secrets of Alchemy*, by Michael Maier which was
described – truly for once – as 'very useful to possess and pleasant to

The notion of a spiritual guide who initiates the seeker into the secrets of creation, is found not only in alchemy but in ancient wisdom literature, and Western mystical texts. Figure 12 from The Book of Lambspring *(in Waite 1893)*

read.' It tells the story of a traveller in search of the miraculous phoenix that would change grief and anger to gold. And some of the famous sequences of visual images and commentaries, such as *The Book of Lambspring*, retain the fresh and spontaneous quality of dream symbolism.

Alchemical accounts of visions may also have influenced a wider field of literature as other writers found in this visionary form a framework for their allegories. We will see in Chapter Five how the visionary aspect of alchemy may have influenced the early forms of opera. Langland's *Piers Plowman*, written in the fourteenth century, begins with the narration of Piers as he falls asleep by the side of the stream:

> And I dreamt a marvellous dream: I was in a wilderness,
> I could not tell where, and looking Eastwards I saw a
> tower high up against the sun, and splendidly built on
> top of a hill; and far beneath it was a great gulf, with a
> dungeon in it, surrounded by deep, dark pits, dreadful
> to see...

Even closer to the alchemical genre is John Bunyan's *Pilgrim's Progress* of 1675, which traces the journey of the pilgrim who wishes to reach salvation and charts the crises and stages of transformation he must go through before reaching the Holy City. It starts:

> As I walked through the wilderness of this world, I
> lighted on a certain place where there was a den, and
> laid me down in that place to sleep; and as I slept, I
> dreamed a dream...

Pilgrim's Progress has a great deal in common with the alchemical process, since it begins with Christian's struggle with the Slough of Despond, the 'scum and filth' of the world, that equates with the base First Matter of the alchemists. It ends, as does the Great Work, with gold, in the Celestial City:

> So I saw that when they awoke [Christian and Hope]
> they addressed themselves to go up to the city. But, as I
> said, the reflection of the sun upon the city (for the city
> was pure gold...) was so extremely glorious, that they
> could not, as yet, with open faces behold it, but through
> an instrument made for that purpose. So I saw that, as
> they went on, there met them two men in raiment that
> shone like gold, also their faces shone as the light...

Chapter Four

Emblems of knowledge:
From Islam to medieval Europe

Alchemy passed from the Greeks and Egyptians to the Arabs, who then transmitted to Europe. From the seventh century onwards the Arabs devoted much time and study not only to alchemy but also to mathematics, astronomy and astrology. The rise of the new religion, Islam, founded by the prophet Mohammed, gave a strong focus for the Arab tribes and enabled them to consolidate their identity; from this new unity arose conditions favourable to learning and experiment. The Arabs expanded their Islamic empire into Spain in the eighth century, and this, though it was the cause of strife, enabled Arabic teachings and ideas to pass more easily into the rest of Europe.

The Arabs translated many ancient alchemical works from the Greek, and certain Greek texts have come down to us today only through their Arabic versions, making it difficult for scholars to verify and date the original material. The most famous Arabian alchemists known to us are Khalid ibn Yazid (died 704), Abu Musa Jabir (flourished 760), and Al-Rhazi (born *circa* 864). **Khalid** was a prince who lived at Damascus, said to have been the first Moslem to take an interest in alchemy and to have been initiated into its secrets by a Christian hermit called Morienus.

Abu Musa Jabir, often called **Geber**, was venerated by the later European alchemists more than any other Arabic writer, and it is probable that a Geber school or tradition carried on his work and used his name to head later texts. Jabir lived in the eighth century; he was a member of a South Arabian tribe who came to Arabia from Persia because of political unrest. Reputedly, he studied with certain important religious leaders of the day and became a Sufi, a member of that mystical and esoteric sect that flourished within Islam. As well as alchemy, he studied medicine, warfare and music, and we know that he found favour at court for much of his life as a respected scholar. His most influential ideas were probably those that modified the Aristotelian theory of the elements.

Geber also introduced some of the Arabian love of numbers into alchemy. He worked out various complicated systems for calculating the right amounts of materials and substances to use in alchemical procedures. He attempted to find the perfect balance of substances and elements and came nearer to the modern principles of chemical equations in his work than any other alchemist of this or later times. About a hundred books are ascribed to him, but it is certain that many of these are pseudographical. Some of the alchemical methods he describes are so complex and tortuous that his name gave rise to the term 'gibberish'. There is a legend that about two hundred years after his death his laboratory at Kufa was discovered as some houses were being demolished, exposing his work room and a golden mortar more than two pounds in weight!

Al-Rhazi, also known as **Rhases,** was born around AD 864, and spent his life chiefly at Ray, near Teheran, with periods of work carried out at Baghdad. He is remembered as a man of great learning, specialising in medicine and alchemy, but also noted for his understanding of philosophy and skill as a musician. His writings on medicine stood the test of time until the sixteenth or seventeenth century, and in his day he was surrounded by many young students and visiting scholars whom he instructed. E. J. Holmyard quotes the following description of his teaching life:

> One of his biographers has drawn a graphic picture of Razi as an old man, seated on the paving of the courtyard of the hospital surrounded by his pupils. The advanced students sat in a ring nearest him, and in outer concentric rings sat those whom we might call the second-year and first-year men. Razi, the fount of wisdom at the centre, expounded to his immediate entourage, and the information, suitably simplified, was passed on to the less experienced. (Holmyard 1957: 87)

His works were great favourites with the European alchemists, even though he was interested primarily in practical chemistry, especially in the classification of substances and in improving laboratory technique.

The alchemical operation

Early European alchemists seized eagerly upon any translations they could acquire of Arabian and Greek alchemical texts. But for them by far and away the most significant early text was the *Emerald Tablet of Hermes Trismegistus*, also called the *Tabula Smaragdina*. This was the alchemists' creed, the affirmation of their work, and a constant source of guidance and wisdom to them. It was sometimes engraved on the walls of the alchemical laboratory, and there can scarcely have been an alchemist who did not have the words written out or committed to memory.

There are several versions of the text, since it is known both in Latin and Arabic, and probably existed in Syriac and Greek forms before that. The translation commonly favoured by present-day scholars is that of R. Steele and D. W. Singer, made early in the twentieth century, which runs as follows:

> True it is, without falsehood, certain and most true. That which is above is like to that which is below, and that which is below is like to that which is above, to accomplish the miracles of one thing.

> And as all things were by the contemplation of one, so all things arose from this one thing by a single act of adaptation.

> The father thereof is the Sun, the mother the Moon.

> The Wind carried it in its womb, the Earth is the nurse thereof.

> It is the father of all works of wonder throughout the whole world.

> The power thereof is perfect.

> If it be cast on to Earth, it will separate the element of Earth from that of Fire, the subtle from the gross.

> With great sagacity it doth ascend gently from Earth to Heaven.

> Again it doth descend to Earth, and uniteth in itself the force from things superior and things inferior.

> Thus thou wilt possess the glory of the brightness of the whole world, and all obscurity will fly from thee.

'The father thereof is the Sun, the mother the Moon', as the Emerald Tablet states. The conception which leads to the birth of gold takes place in the alchemical bath. (Emblem 34, Michael Maier, Atlanta Fugiens, *1617.)*

This thing is the strong fortitude of all strength, for it overcometh every subtle thing and doth penetrate every solid substance.

Thus was this world created.

Hence will there be marvellous adaptations achieved, of which the manner is this.

For this reason I am called Hermes Trismegistus, because I hold three parts of the wisdom of the whole world.

That which I had to say about the operation of Sol is completed.

This text probably originates from the early centuries of the Christian era, in common with other writings ascribed to Hermes (see page 116). But the European alchemists believed that the words came from the very dawn of time, and were the original revelation of alchemy to man through the divine person of Hermes Trismegistus:

> Hermes saw the totality of things. Having seen he understood. Having understood, he had the power to reveal and show. And indeed what he knew, he wrote down. What he wrote, he mostly hid away, keeping silence rather than speaking out, so that every generation coming into the world had to seek out these things.

(From the *Corpus Hermeticum*, quoted by Lindsay 1970)

The name Hermes Trismegistus means 'Hermes the Thrice Great'. In the general evolution of the classical deities, Hermes later became known as Mercury; but though Hermes and Mercury play somewhat similar roles in alchemy, they are not identical. Hermes was seen as the source of alchemical knowledge and was often thought to have been a real, though semi-divine, Egyptian adept. Mercury was the representation of the living spirit of alchemy, the volatile transforming power that could exalt matter into its most refined state; we shall return to him shortly.

The enigmatic character of the Emerald Tablet, and indeed the trickster qualities of Hermes and Mercury, are reflected in alchemical literature of all periods. Alchemical texts and illustrations are fascinating, but they are also tantalising, cryptic, and sometimes deliberately misleading in their descriptions. How true the alchemical aphorism: 'Many search; few find'. Sometimes, even if the secret could be found, it was too late; after working for sixty years, the aged seeker, Tonsile, met an initiate only to be rebuffed thus:

> Tonsile said I, what should it you avail
> Such a thing to know? your limbs doth you fail
> For very age, therefore cease your lay;
> And love your beads, it is high time to pray;
> For if you knew the materials of our stone
> Ere you could make it your days would be gone.

(Norton 1477)

The influence of the Arabian alchemists may well be felt in the labelling of the stages of the process which these medieval and later

Mercury is sometimes described as a double agent. Here the two Mercuries must be joined, like with like, according to alchemical principles. (Emblem 10, Michael Maier, Atlanta Fugiens, *1617.)*

European alchemists used. As well as emblematic pictures and mythological descriptions, the stages were given titles relating more closely to the chemical operations that were carried out. These act as a reminder that alchemy had a nitty-gritty physical side to it, however important the spiritual process. *The Sum of Perfection*, attributed to Geber, but probably by an early medieval author, lists the stages as: sublimation, descension, distillation, calcination, solution, coagulation, fixation and ceration. These involve processes we would recognise in physical terms as heating, condensation, evaporation, and so on. Lest it should be thought that with one such key we have swiftly arrived at the heart of the alchemical secret, it should be immediately pointed out that no two such descriptions of the process ever agreed! Even the number of stages varied, often set between seven and twelve, linking in to other symbolic correspondences such as the seven days of creation or the twelve signs of the zodiac. George Ripley, a fifteenth century alchemist, called the operation The Twelve Gates and likened it to a circular castle with twelve entrances, each signifying a stage of the process. These were named as: calcination, solution, separation, conjunction, putrefaction, congelation, cibation, sublimation, fermentation, exaltation, multiplication and projection. We can make connections between the chemical and symbolical significance of some of these, for instance the conjunction signifying combining sulphur and mercury in the vessel and the marriage of the king and queen. Putrefaction, the stage that follows, indicates that the united bodies must be killed by heat so that regeneration may follow, which corresponds to the death, the blackening, whose symbol is the raven.

The primal material

The alchemist must take some substance to start his operations. But what should his 'first matter' be? This is one of the most jealously guarded secrets of alchemy. However, since the perfect Stone is to be created from something that is apparently base and worthless, the matter required is often described as being overlooked and despised by men – 'the corner stone which the builders rejected'. The baser forms of alchemy, especially in the Middle Ages, took this as a sign that any particularly nasty substance would do, such as 'poudres diverse, asshes, dong, pisse, and cley' (Chaucer, *The Canon Yeoman's Tale*), not to mention blood, hair, bones and spittle. The more sophisticated alchemists poured scorn upon this practice, and implied that the first material is no common substance, but a mysterious ingredient of the universe. It is:

> ... familiar to all men, both young and old, is found in the country, in the village, in the town, in all things created by God; yet it is despised by all. Rich and poor handle it every day. It is cast into the street by servant maids. Children play with it. Yet no one prizes it, though, next to the human soul, it is the most beautiful and the most precious thing upon earth and has the power to pull down kings and princes. Nevertheless, it is esteemed the vilest and meanest of earthly things.

(From *Gloria Mundi* [1526] quoted by Read 1936)

Some authorities consider that in the early days of alchemy, the black Egyptian silt with its tremendous fertility may have provided the idea of a base substance with great nourishing and creative powers. Whether or not this is true, by the sixteenth and seventeenth centuries, the concept had become much more complex. Some writers imply that the primal material is metallic, because it is impossible to create gold from anything that does not have a metallic root; but they also hint that its form does not resemble what we usually think of as metal. And in some texts the distinction between the primal material and the Stone itself, the end product of the process, is hard to define; the implication seems to be that the Stone is released from the base material by the alchemical process and is already indwelling in it when the alchemist takes it up:

> This Matter is found in one thing, out of which alone
> our Stone is prepared ... without any foreign admixture;
> and its quality, appearance, and properties have been
> set forth in the following manner. It is composed of
> three things, yet it is only one... They also call it the
> universal Magnesia, or the seed of the world, from
> which all natural objects take their origin. Its properties
> are of a singular kind; for, in addition to its marvellous
> nature and form, it is neither hot and dry like fire, nor
> cold and wet like water, nor cold and dry like earth, but
> a perfect preparation of all the elements... With respect
> to its outward appearance, figure, form, and shape, they
> call it a stone, and not a stone... It is found potentially
> everywhere, and in everything, but in all its perfection
> and fullness only in one thing... By the ignorant and the
> beginner it is thought to be the vilest and meanest of
> things. It is sought by many Sages, and found by few;
> suspected by those that are far away, and received by
> those that are near; seen by all, but known by few...

(From *The Sophic Hydrolith* in Waite 1893)

The primal material is also associated with the Ouroboros, the circular serpent with its tail in its mouth. This goes back to the dawn of alchemy, for in an early Greek text we read:

> Here is the mystery: The serpent Ouroboros [biting his
> tail] is the composition which in our [work] is devoured
> and melted, dissolved and transformed by fermentation.
> It becomes dark green from which the golden colour
> derives. It is from this which the red comes, called the
> colour of cinnabar; it is the cinnabar of the
> philosophers.

Its stomach and its back are the colour of saffron; its head is dark green, its four legs are the four imperfect metals [lead, copper, tin, iron]; its three ears are the three sublimated vapours [perhaps salt, mercury and sulphur].

> The One gives to the Other its blood; and the One
> engenders the Other. Nature rejoices in nature; nature
> charms nature; nature triumphs over nature; and nature
> masters nature; and this is not from one nature opposing
> another, but through the one and same nature, through
> the alchemical process, with care and great effort.

(Translated from Berthelot 1888)

In the *Gold Making of Cleopatra* (*circa* AD 100) the Ouroboros is drawn and the text reads: 'One is the All and by it the All and in it the All and if it does not contain the All it is nothing.' Although the later alchemists, especially in the seventeenth century, brought the philosophy of their work to the heights of sophistication, yet they still based their operations on the simplicity and unity of this premise. Transformation comes primarily through purifying and perfecting the original material. This is a declaration of faith, that the divine spark dwells in every single atom that exists, however corrupt and base it may appear to our eyes.

Mercury

The alchemical serpent, or dragon, is closely connected with Mercury, the transforming agent of the alchemical process. Mercury is released and activated from the primal material, and is then transformed, fixed, and brought to perfection through the operations. Appropriately enough for such an elusive and volatile figure, alchemical descriptions of him – or her, for it is often stated that the Mercurial force is a feminine one – blend into definitions of the first material, the Stone, and 'our gold'. 'Our Mercury' is not 'common mercury', the alchemists are quick to point out. Charles Nicholl, in *The Chemical Theatre*, grapples with these problems admirably:

> There are two directions in which alchemical Mercury
> leads us. On the one hand, it is a complex elaboration
> of chemical substance, its various qualities referring
> back to the properties of quicksilver, or 'common
> mercury'... But there is another direction entirely, away
> from chemical matter. Mercury is not, finally, a
> substance, or even many substances: it is a process... All
> these [alchemical writings] point to one crucial idea:
> that transformation is something intrinsic and contained

Ouroboros, the serpent or dragon with its tail in its mouth, a key image in alchemy. (Emblem 14 Michael Maier, Atlanta Fugiens, *1617.)*

> inside matter... Each stage of this self-devouring, self-generating process bears the name 'Mercury'. Mercury, in short, is alchemy itself.

> (Nicholl 1980)

In his *Alchemical Studies*, C. G. Jung quotes from *Aurelia Occulta*, which is contained in the *The Chemical Theatre*:

> I am the poison-dripping dragon, who is everywhere and can be cheaply had. That upon which I rest, and that which rests upon me, will be found within me by those who pursue their investigations in accordance with the rules of the Art. My water and fire destroy and put together; from my body you may extract the green lion and the red. But if you do not have exact knowledge of me, you will destroy your five senses with my fire. From my snout there comes a spreading poison

The dragon is a symbol of latent power in alchemy, and is sometimes equated with Mercury. Its blood must be shed to fuel the process of transformation. (From a German alchemical poem, seventeenth century MS. Add. A. 287, p104, The Bodleian Library, University of Oxford.)

that has brought death to many. Therefore you should skilfully separate the coarse from the fine, if you do not wish to suffer utter poverty. I bestow on you the powers of the male and the female, and also those of heaven and of earth. The mysteries of my art must be handled with courage and greatness of mind if you would conquer me by the power of fire, for already very many have come to grief, their riches and labour lost. I am the egg of nature, known only to the wise... By the philosophers I am named Mercurius; my spouse is the [philosophic] gold; I am the old dragon, found everywhere on the globe of the earth, father and mother, young and old, very strong and very weak, death and resurrection, visible and invisible, hard and soft; I descend into the earth and ascend to the heavens, I am the highest and the lowest, the lightest and the heaviest; often the order of nature is reversed in me, as regards colour, number, weight and measure; I contain the light of nature; I am dark and light; I come forth from heaven and earth; I am known and yet do not exist at all; by virtue of the sun's rays all colours shine in me and all metals. I am the carbuncle of the sun, the most noble purified earth, through which you may change copper, iron, tin, and lead into gold.

Another emblem showing how the Dragon must be slain to release its vital powers. (Emblem 25, Michael Maier, Atlanta Fugiens, 1617.)

On a lighter note, Mercury can be found in conversation with an alchemist in *The New Chemical Light* by Michael Sendivogius (Waite 1893). A foolish alchemist has read that he should start his work with Mercury; he tries to heat common quicksilver which evaporates, where upon he accuses his wife of stealing it. Then he tries again, adding all sorts of substances to it such as 'herbs, urine and vinegar' to see if he can do any better. Failing with these, he remembers reading that the dung hill is the place to seek, so he starts to use dung, but all ends badly. Then, in a dream, a wise old man tells him to use the 'Mercury of the Sages'. He manages to conjure up Mercury in person, and tries to wrest the secret from him, but Mercury, true to form, is mischievous and avoids all the alchemist's attempts to force him into submission:

> *Alchemist*: I conjure you by the living God – are you
> not the Mercury of the Sages?

Mercury (pretending to speak in a whimpering and frightened tone of voice): Master, I am Mercury.

Alchemist: Why would you not obey me then? Why could I not fix you?

Mercury: Oh, most high and mighty Master, I implore you to spare your miserable slave! I did not know that you were such a potent philosopher.

Alchemist: Oh, could you not guess as much from the philosophical way in which I operated on you ... (To the Mercury, in awful tones of thunder): Now mind that you obey me, else it will be the worse for you.

Mercury: Gladly, Master, if I can: for I am very weak.

Alchemist: Oho, do you begin to make excuses already?

Mercury: No, but I am very languid.

Alchemist: What is the matter with you?

Mercury: An Alchemist is the matter with me.

Alchemist: Are you laughing at me, you false rogue?

Mercury: Oh, no, no, Master, as God shall spare me, I spoke of an Alchemist – *you* are a philosopher...

Alchemist: Well, I won't praise myself, but I certainly am a learned man. My wife says so too. She always calls me a profoundly learned philosopher.

Mercury: I quite believe you. For philosophers are men whom too much learning and thought have made mad.

Alchemist: Tell me, what am I to do with you? How am I to make you into the Philosopher's Stone?

Mercury: Oh, my master philosopher, that I cannot tell. You are a philosopher, I am the philosopher's humble slave. Whatever he wishes to make me, I become, as far as my nature will allow.

Alchemist: That is all very fine, but I repeat that you must tell me how to treat you, and whether you can become the Philosopher's Stone.

Mercury: Mr Philosopher, if you know, you can make it, and if you don't you can't...

Elemental symbols

We have already looked at the basic role of the four elements in alchemy, and the qualities associated with them. Their specific functions in alchemy, however, though often obscure and mysterious, have interesting images and associations attached to them. The most important ideas concerning earth have been considered in the section on the primal material, but earth may also be represented by creatures such as the deer and the unicorn. Fishes are the creatures of water, birds of air, and salamanders of fire. Fire is mainly an external force in alchemy; the alchemist tends his furnace scrupulously, and must apply the right degree of heat for the different stages of the operation. Often the heat is to be moderate, like that of a chicken giving warmth to her eggs. The period of gestation, after the 'seed' of the Stone has been engendered and remains in the tightly-sealed vessel to come to term, is sustained by the application of fire.

Often a term of forty days is mentioned for the gestation period, and this corresponds to the forty week term for human gestation. Heat, therefore, is seen as a natural medium for growth, as Stolcius writes:

> Here is our warm fire,
> Humid, lovely, and not dangerous;
> That preserves all things,
> And permits none to spoil.
> It is even and good,
> Agreeable to things to be born:
> It carries everything properly heated
> Away with the moisture.
>
> (From Stolcius, *The Pleasure Garden of Chemistry*
> [1624], in Allen 1968: 555)

There are often hints that a substance undergoing transformation must yield up its secret fire, which will help to give the Stone its final power. The Salamander must be brought from his cave:

> [The Salamander] is caught and pierced
> So that it dies and yields up its life with its blood.
> But this, too, happens for its good:
> For from its blood it wins immortal life,
> And then death has no more power over it.
>
> (From *The Book of Lambspring* in Waite 1893)

Water is closely associated with Mercury. It is the universal solvent, and can also be considered as helping to give the right colour to the substance at different stages of the operation – black, white, yellow or red. We have already seen how colour was considered to be a kind of spirit, with special properties and powers. It is also necessary to remember that all the elements were thought to have a higher form, which was quite different from that of normal earth, water, fire and air, and it is probably these special forms which are known as 'our fire' and 'our water'. 'Our Pontic and Catholic water... is sweet, beautiful clear, limpid, and brighter than gold, silver, carbuncles, or diamonds'; 'Our water is a water which does not wet the hands; it is a heavenly water, and yet not rain water'; 'Our water is serene, crystalline, pure and beautiful'.

Sometimes 'our water' is said to be generated from the first matter; sometimes it must be added to the transforming substance to bathe it, nourish it, or colour it.

> The Water of the Wise Men
>
> When a woman mixes
> Colouring with water,
> She is about to wash
> Linen or clothes.
> The water leaves the material
> When it is dried in the open air;
> But the coloured cloth
> Retains the desired colour.
> Likewise the water of the Wise
> Penetrates all large and small metals:
> Use it
> And it tinctures things speedily.
>
> (From Stolcius, *The Pleasure Garden of Chemistry*
> [1624], in Allen 1968: 546)

Bathing and washing was thus called 'woman's work' in alchemy. Sometimes, too, 'our water' is described as a sharp, acidic liquid capable of dissolving any gold or metal that is to be added to the mixture, and in this capacity may go under the name of the Green Dragon. Some writers on alchemy had equated this with *aqua fortis* or *aqua regia* (nitro-hydrochloric acid), acids which would certainly dissolve metal, and we do know that the alchemists had knowledge of these and other powerful chemical substances. But, again, many of the alchemists are at pains to tell us not to confuse the dissolving liquid

The Salamander, a mythical creature said to thrive in the depths of the fire. (Emblem 29, Michael Maier, Atlanta Fugiens, *1617.)*

with ordinary fluids or acids. The more practically orientated alchemists and the dabblers would have used all kinds of chemical compounds in their work; but the fact remains that that in its fullest expression alchemy relied on certain specially prepared substances or elements that were considered to have properties of an extraordinary nature, not to be compared with normal preparations.

A kind of water that is given particular importance in alchemical texts is dew. A famous plate from the *Mutus Liber* of 1667 shows a male and a female alchemist wringing out into a bowl dew that they have gathered by exposing large sheets of cloth to the air. Dew might be used to moisten the alchemical matter, to bathe it or to nourish it. What would make dew so special? There are two schools of thought on this. Some alchemists, such as Armand Barbault, the twentieth-century French alchemist, consider dew to be permeated with the living vitality of the plants from which it is gathered; it thus imparts a 'green fire' – an enriching food – to the matter. Others see dew as descending from the atmosphere, a mystical medium, the receptacle of celestial influences. In the *Zohar* (a collection of Kabbalistic writings dating from medieval times), dew is mentioned as a holy attribute:

> v. 47 – And it is written, Isa xxvi. 19: 'The dew of the lights is thy dew.' Of the lights – that is, from the brightness of the Ancient One.
>
> 48 – And by that dew are nourished the holy supernal ones.
>
> 49 – And this is that manna which is prepared for the just in the world to come.
>
> 50 – And that dew distilleth upon the ground of the holy apple trees ...
>
> *51* – And the appearance of this dew is white, like unto the colour of the crystal stone, whose appearance hath all colours in itself.

(Translation by MacGregor Mathers 1970: 116)

The element of air is related to the emblem of birds, which occur in many different forms in alchemical texts. A whole book could be devoted just to the symbolism of the different birds in alchemy (McLean 1979). The appearance of the raven or crow symbolizes the *nigredo*, or putrefaction of the first material. A white bird, such as the swan, or dove, may refer to the first time that the 'soul' of the matter is released, the matter having polarized into the black of the raven and the white of the more elevated bird. The peacock has the quality of a herald, for with the arrival of the Peacock's Tail, the show of beautiful iridescent colours in the vessel, the alchemist knows that his work is empowered and that the transformation is under way. The pelican is represented in connection with the legend that the pelican fed her young with the blood of her own breast, which relates to the idea that the first matter contained in itself all that it needed for transformation and perfection, including its own nourishment: this is similar to the concept of the secret 'water' being extracted from the substance and then fed back to it to help it grow. The eagle has a close association with Mercury, and two eagles shown fighting each other refer to the internal battle that takes place in the initial stages to untie the knot which binds the elements together. The eagle exalted or poised in the

'Go to the woman washing sheets, and do thou likewise.' Washing
the matter in the alchemical vessel to purify, moisten or dissolve as
necessary. *(Emblem 3, Michael Maier,* Atlanta Fugiens, *1617.)*

air is Mercury in his most sublime state, emblem of inspiration and
knowledge, frequently a sign that the work is completed.

In *The Chemical Wedding of Christian Rosenkreutz,* published in
1690, a long alchemical allegory concerning an initiate's quest to be
accepted and present at a royal wedding, there is a description of the
alchemical process in terms of a bird that emerges from an egg,
changes colour and shape, and is sacrificed for its blood:

> Our Egg being now ready was taken out; But it needed
> no cracking, for the Bird that was in it soon freed
> himself, and shewed himself very jocond, yet he looked
> very Bloody and unshapen... The Bird grew so fast
> under our eyes, that we well saw why the Virgin gave
> us such a warning of him. He bit and scratcht so

devillishly about him, that could he have had his will upon any of us, he would have soon dispatched him. Now he was wholly black, and wild, wherefore other meat was brought to him... whereupon all his black Feathers moulted again, and instead of them there grew out Snow-white Feathers. He was somewhat tamer too, and suffered himself to be more tractable, nevertheless we did not trust him. At the third feeding his Feathers began to be so curiously coloured, that in all my Life I never saw the like colours for Beauty. He was also exceeding tame, and behaved himself so friendly with us, that (the Virgin consenting) we released him from his Captivity.

(Allen 1968: 145)

The images and symbols of alchemy helped to show the profundity of the alchemical operation. The alchemist saw his work as a great mystery, as a way of penetrating to the heart of the created world. He took nothing for granted; he did not treat his laboratory operations as mechanical repetitions but as a living process in which he must participate. He aimed to go beyond the realm of normal appearances and effects, to the causes of those effects, where he might glimpse 'Venus unveiled' in her chamber – an experience so intense and powerful that it was considered highly dangerous if the alchemist was not inwardly prepared. An analogous situation might be if the atomic physicist suddenly began to experience and perceive everything at the atomic level. Normal concepts of solidity, shape and identity would cease to have meaning; it is not difficult to see that the experience could be a totally overwhelming unless one was prepared and trained for it, emotionally and mentally, irrespective of how much 'atomic theory' one knew in advance.

The celestial influence

The relationship of the Earth to the solar system and to the stars was considered very important in alchemy. In fact, until the eighteenth century, it was accepted by the majority of people that the celestial bodies were animate and possessed of particular qualities that affected life on Earth. The accompanying assumption was that they were instruments, or agents of the Divine Will, and sometimes (more immediately) the tools of Nature, governing the growth of everything upon earth, including metals. The following quotation indicates the power of Nature and the part played by the planets:

Battle of opposites: here dog and wolf fight, representing the warring forces of alchemy. (Emblem 47, Michael Maier, Atlanta Fugiens, *1617.)*

By my wisdom I govern the first principle of motion. My hands are the eighth sphere, as my Father ordained; my hammers are the seven planets with which I forge beautiful things. The substance out of which I fashion all my works, and all things under heaven, I obtain from the four elements alone... By my virtue and efficacy I make the imperfect perfect, whether it be a metal or a human body. I mix its ingredients, and temper the four elements. I reconcile opposites, and calm their Discord.

This is the golden chain which I have linked together of my heavenly virtues and earthly substances.

(John A. Mehung, *A Demonstration of Nature,* seventeenth century, in Waite 1893)

The egg is a symbol of primal unity, similar to Ouroboros, the serpent with the tail in its mouth. In alchemy it must either be coaxed into hatching, or else split open to initiate the process of transformation. (Emblem 8, Michael Maier, Atlanta Fugiens, *1617.)*

Each metal was said to correspond to a particular planet, and when that planet was strong in influence, the 'growth' of the metal would be accelerated within the earth. The influence could be assessed astrologically, by examining the relationship of the planets to one another and studying their position in relation to the signs of the zodiac for the time in question. The association of planets with metals was precise, and related to the active principle of the planet as defined astrologically or mythologically. Saturn, for instance, considered to be slow, profound, weighty, had the correspondence of lead, the heaviest of the metals concerned. Venus, planet of ease, pleasure, beauty and malleability, corresponded to copper, a soft and gleaming metal. The sun corresponded to gold, the moon to silver, Mercury to quicksilver, Mars to iron, and Jupiter to tin. The alchemist would need to know and understand these correspondences well, since it was common to try and prepare elixirs of the other metals apart from silver and gold,

Some of the planets pictured in symbolic form: left to right, Saturn, Moon, Mercury and Mars. Each planet represents a metal in alchemy. (From a German alchemical poem, seventeenth century. MS. Add. A. 287, p106, The Bodleian Library, University of Oxford.)

especially as medicinal remedies. Often in the alchemical texts one will find the metals called by the names of the planets themselves.

Since Nature was said to operate through the medium of the planets, the alchemist, seeking to use art to accelerate and perfect the natural processes, must understand and utilise the principles of stellar influences. Many alchemists, therefore, were skilled astrologers, and it was common to select a favourable time astrologically to begin the Great Work. The initiation of new stages of the process might also be governed by astrological conditions. It was generally considered that the work was best begun at or around the vernal equinox, when the sun moves into the sign of Aries, the first point of the Zodiac. However, more elaborate calculations and assessments were frequently employed, just as a gardener might have it in mind to sow certain seeds in a particular week, but would vary the timing according to prevalent weather and ground conditions.

Alchemists perpetuated the view that the cosmos is whole and alive and that all its components have spirit and purpose; the stars and the planets provide a 'field' of energy that man can either experience passively or use actively for creative purposes. The alchemist therefore cannot work against the natural and stellar influences, but he can channel them to bring about transformation:

> Let me sum up in a few words what I have to say. The substance is of heavenly birth, its life is preserved by the

63

stars, and nourished by the four elements; then it must
perish, and be putrefied; again, by the influence of the
stars, which works through the elements, it is restored to
life, and becomes once more a heavenly thing that has
its habitation in the highest region of the firmament.
Then you will find that the heavenly has assumed an
earthly body, and that the earthly body has been
reduced to a heavenly substance.

(From *The Golden Tripod* in Waite 1893)

The alchemist: image and reality

What image does the word 'alchemist' conjure up? Perhaps that of a
lean and bearded figure, dressed in a dark and dusty cloak, muttering
mysterious incantations as he leans over his cauldrons and bubbling
retorts. When the history of alchemy is studied, it soon becomes
obvious that this picture is far from the truth, but it must also be noted
that even in its heyday alchemy was considered a subject for ridicule.
The majority of people were not well informed about alchemical aims
and practices, partly because most serious alchemists kept very much
to themselves, and those who did pronounce themselves publicly to be
alchemists were often the most fraudulent or foolish practitioners of all.
It is from their activities that the popular image of alchemy derives.

> Their clothes be bawdy and worn threadbare,
> Men may smell them for multipliers where they go;
> To file their fingers with corrosives they do not spare
> Their eyes be bleryd, and their cheeks both lean and
> blue...
> They search for the stone in soot, dung, urine, wine,
> blood, eggs.
> To see their houses it is a noble sport,
> What furnaces, what glasses there be of divers shape;
> What salts, what powders, what oils, and waters fort,
> How eloquently, de materia prima, they clape
> And yet to find the truth they have no hap.

(Ripley, *The Compound of Alchemy*, in Ashmole 1652)

Many came to ruin through their search for the stone, addicted to the
quest for gold and spending all their time and money in fruitless
experiment. The unsuccessful experimenters were characterised by a
stink of brimstone, worn-out clothes, an unhealthy tinge to the skin

An alchemist's laboratory. Notice the caduceus or double serpent shape, a physical representation of Mercury's emblem (see the illustration of the double Mercury on page 47).

and a general air of poverty. The charlatans could be distinguished by their bragging and boasting, their readiness to talk about the art of alchemy and their willingness to promise spectacular transmutations; they often lived a wandering life – for obvious reasons.

Going beyond the superficial picture, though, we find quite different types of people seriously involved in the study of alchemy. In medieval times these were often monks, but both then and later the aspirants included noblemen, men of business, men of learning – and a few women. All had to have enough time and money to support their researches, for there were likely to be months and even years of long experiment and the alchemist had to be committed to regulating the fire, mixing, adding, and, above all, to waiting and watching for the right reactions in the vessel.

In medieval times the monastic environment provided excellent opportunities for alchemical work. Monasteries were natural centres of learning, since all books were written in manuscript form and one of the chief occupations of monks was in copying out and illuminating the texts. Many monasteries had fine libraries, and received visitors from afar bringing new insights from other teachers and countries.

We find many traces of monastic alchemists. In Elias Ashmole's anthology of alchemical poetry, *Theatrum Chemicum Britannicum,* published in 1652 we find a contribution from the rather sinister-sounding 'Pearce, the Black Monk', who had a fair talent for verse, the style of which would seem to place him in the medieval period:

> I am Mercury the mighty flower,
> I am most worthy of honour;
> I am source of Sol, Luna and Mars,
> I am settler of Saturn, and source of Venus,
> I am Empress, Princess, and Regal of Queens,
> I am Mother of Mirror, and maker of light,
> I am head and highest and fairest in sight...

John Dastin, a member of an austere monastic order, is remembered for his courageous fight to keep the name of alchemy untarnished. He lived in the first half of the fourteenth century, at a time when Pope John XXII had condemned alchemy because of the proliferation of fraudulent practitioners. He passed an edict by which those caught counterfeiting gold and silver had to repay the equivalent sum of money back into the common treasury; persistent offenders had their goods confiscated and were branded as criminals: offending clerics were to be deprived of their livings. Dastin wrote both to the Pope and to Cardinal Orsini assuring them that there was more to alchemy than deception, and maintained that it was within the possibilities of nature to prepare the alchemical elixir. The Pope may have been dazzled by such erudition; at any rate, Dastin does not seem to have suffered for his efforts; and E.J. Holmyard tells us that when the Pope died, he left an enormous fortune that was reputed to be of alchemical origin!

The most famous alchemical monk is **Sir George Ripley,** who came of an aristocratic family and was a canon regular in the Augustinian priory at Bridlington, in Yorkshire. This priory had a strong tradition of learning and in the fifteenth century Ripley made it the base for his alchemical experiments, apparently antagonising the other inhabitants by the smells and fumes that were generated in his laboratory. One interesting feature of Ripley's alchemical education is that he spent some time in Rhodes, as a guest of the Knights of St John of Jerusalem. Rhodes had been occupied by the Knights since 1310, and quickly gained a reputation for being a cosmopolitan centre of learning, a little like a latter-day Alexandria. The Knights' community, though based on Catholic principles, was receptive to innovatory ideas that would have been suspect elsewhere, and many came to Rhodes to teach and learn in an atmosphere of comparative intellectual freedom.

Since one of the chief occupations of the Knights of St John was healing the sick, there was a natural connection between their endeavours to promote the study of medicine and herbalism, and alchemy, whose Elixir had the reputation of being a panacea. In the late medieval period, Jacques Millac, a French herbalist and apothecary who had antagonised the Catholic Church in his own country because of his interest in alchemy, joined the Order in order to be able to live in Rhodes and experiment as he wished. A university had been established there that was noted for its teaching of medicine, while a special school for apothecaries was attached to the hospital run by the Knights. Another noted alchemist, **Bernard of Treves** (who probably lived in the fourteenth century) completed his alchemical studies on Rhodes, where it is said that he met a 'man of religion' whose alchemical library was attractive enough to keep him there for eight years.

In the fifteenth century Ripley followed Bernard's precedent, gained at least some of his alchemical expertise during a stay on Rhodes. Ripley became well-known for such works as *The Compound of Alchemy* (containing the famous passage on the Twelve Gates), which quickly became established as alchemical classics. With Ripley, a link is formed between the clerical and the secular alchemist, for **Thomas Norton,** a well-to-do Bristol merchant, claimed that Ripley was his teacher. Norton, who may also have held the post of Privy Councillor to Edward IV, published his work *The Ordinal of Alchemy* anonymously in 1477. However, despite the appearance of discretion and modesty, he plainly had hopes that someone would recognise his hand in the work, as he concealed his name in an easy cipher which revealed the motto:

> Thomas Norton of Briseto
> A parfet Master ye maie him trowe.

Thomas Charnock, born around 1524, was also taught alchemy by monks. His profession is not known and he had little education, though this did not deter him from the search. His own account of his work (in Ashmole 1652) is full of zest and frankness, and he was plainly pleased with his own verse. He recounts how he meets a blind friar who tells him that he will only teach the alchemical art to a most gifted and wonderful young man that he has heard of called Charnock! His virtues are apparently such that 'Wherefore his knowledge, gravity and wit, He may well be crowned Poet Laureate.'

Charnock suffered several set-backs in his alchemical work. The most infuriating came when he was called up to fight at Calais:

> When I saw there was none other boot
> But that I must go spite of my heart took root;
> In my fury I took a hatchet in my hand,
> And brake all my work whereas it did stand,
> And as for my pots I knocked them together,
> And also my glasses into many a shiver...

From the sixteenth century onwards alchemy became a magnet for men of learning, especially those seeking a comprehensive knowledge of the universe. Their creed was that there should be no boundaries between arts, sciences, mysticism and occult knowledge. Each discipline was seen both as a valid way of gaining knowledge about the created world and of learning to operate within it. A metaphysical understanding would both help to explain physical phenomena and inspire practical inventions. Yet, though alchemy was taken seriously by those of considerable intellectual reputation, it certainly never found universal favour. Some were simply sceptical of alchemical claims but others saw in alchemy and occult arts the machinations of the devil.

John Dee (1527–1608), a controversial Elizabethan figure, was suspected of being a sorcerer when he invented an elaborate mechanical beetle for a stage play that gave the illusion of flying! Dee was a remarkable man who took a keen interest in alchemy; in later life he had laboratories built at his house in Mortlake. He was a favourite of Queen Elizabeth, who consulted him as to a suitable astrological date and time for her coronation. Dee was well-versed in mechanics, optics, navigation, history and mathematics and was far-sighted enough to propose a national scheme for the preservation of ancient monuments and a national 'Library Royal'. He took a special interest in clairvoyance and is often remembered for his association with the dubious Edward Kelley, who acted as a scryer for him in his attempts to communicate with the world of spirits and angels. But Dee was not the unquestioning dupe that some authorities have assumed, for his diaries show that he was often critical of Kelley. However, he found certain qualities or psychic abilities in Kelley that he valued, and together they tried both crystal gazing and dowsing for hidden

John Dee pictured with Edward Kelley in, raising the spirits of the dead, a fictitious and sensationalised version of his magical practices. (The Astrologer of the Nineteenth Century, 1825)

treasure. Dee and Kelley went to Poland together, where they undertook to demonstrate alchemical transformation to the Emperor of Bohemia; but the attempt failed and they were dismissed in a state of near poverty after which they parted company – with Kelley devoting himself to alchemy, and Dee becoming Warden of Christ's College, Manchester. Dee was never happy thereafter, especially after the death of Queen Elizabeth, for James I was unsympathetic to any activities associated with magic or alchemy.

In the sixteenth and seventeenth centuries an interest in alchemy was apparent in the highest circles in both England and Scotland. As Adam McLean writes:

> Now at that time in Scotland there was quite a
> flourishing alchemical school probably centred around
> Napier, including the Earl of Argyll, perhaps William
> Drummond of Hawthornden the poet, Patrick Ruthven
> (who was at the time imprisoned in the Tower of
> London and was part of the Tower Group of Alchemists
> which included the Earl of Northumberland, Henry
> Percy, Sir Walter Raleigh, and Thomas Hariot). Another

important Scottish alchemist of the period was Sir
George Erskine, who was very close to King James... Sir
George Erskine's alchemical manuscripts, a large part of
which still survive, indicate his broad reading in the
alchemical tradition, there being scarcely an important
alchemical work that is not included in his collections.

(McLean 1981b: 27)

John Napier (1550–1617), better known as the inventor of logarithms,
was a serious student of alchemy who was instructed and helped by a
German alchemist, bold Daniel Muller. Muller had a great influence
upon the Scottish school of alchemists and some of the letters he wrote
explaining the alchemical process in allegorical terms still survive. For
instance, a copy of a letter sent to the Earl of Argyll begins:

Right Honourable

Your earnest desire to profit in the study of metaphysical
philosophy, I thought it good to give your Lordship a
taste of such marrow as I have by God's assistance
sucked out of the bones of old philosophy...

He describes the alchemical work as needing the living blood of 'a
most ugly, venomous, and horrid flying Dragon' who dwells in 'the
hidden caverns of one huge mountain '. (This is probably a reference
to the powerful and volatile Mercury concealed in an unpleasant
substance of metallic origin.) As is often the case, the appearance of
such an alchemical adept upon the scene is mysterious; we do not
know whether Muller was sent for, or whether he came of his own
volition; nor do we know who his associates were in Germany.

Many accounts of the lives of alchemists have been passed down
without proper investigation, and undoubtedly several of them are
distortions of the truth or even complete inventions. *The Testament of
Cremer* claims to be the story of an Abbot Cremer of Westminster, who
was instructed in alchemy by Ramon Lull. Cremer introduces Lull to
the king (Edward III) and Lull promises to make gold for the king if the
king himself will go to war against the Turks and use some of the gold
for enriching a monastic house. The gold was duly made, it is said, but
the king broke his promise, leaving 'that holy man sore afflicted in
spirit'. However, no record exists of any Abbot Cremer, there is no
proof that Lull was an alchemist and the 'rose nobles' coins are said to
have been struck from the alchemical gold, are anachronisms.

Women in alchemy

Women have played a less prominent part in alchemy than men. Plainly, the demands of an art that required constant and prolonged attention made it impossible for most women to pursue it seriously, for it would not fit in easily with child-bearing or with the running of a household. However, certain women alchemists are known to have existed; some husbands and wives worked together, and further research may bring to light accounts of more women who were interested in alchemy. We have already seen that Maria the Jewess and Kleopatra were noted alchemists of antiquity. Zosimos, the Greek alchemist, had a sister called Theosebeia who was involved in alchemy, but we only know of her existence through fragments of letters that Zosimos wrote to her. Later times have no well-known lady alchemists on record, but it is possible that they were overlooked both by historians and contemporary alchemists. There are a few brief references: John Aubrey (the seventeenth-century historian) mentions that Mary Sidney (the wife of the Earl of Pembroke) was 'a great chymist, and spent yearly a great deale in that study'. Lady Anne Conway (1642–84) has already been cited as being highly influential in the Rosicrucian circle of the period, whose members would have included alchemy as one of their chief studies.

A theme that is shadowy to unravel, but in some ways more interesting to contemplate, is of man and woman working together in 'the Great Work'. The process of alchemy depends upon correct understanding of the male and female principles inherent in matter (sulphur and mercury), of separating them and uniting them in harmony, and it is therefore readily understandable that the alchemists would have sought to echo this idea in their own work. In certain pictures and accounts we find the idea that both the man and the woman had something vital to contribute to the operation. Illustrations in the *Mutus Liber* of 1677 show a man and a woman working together to gather dew, tend the vessel and the furnace, and assist each other in almost every stage of the process. The illustrations show precisely the different actions performed by each of the pair. In one illustration, they kneel on each side of the furnace; the man has his hands folded and his head bowed in prayer while the woman gazes upwards, lifting one arm high in a graceful gesture of blessing. Armand Barbault, a noted twentieth-century alchemist, always worked in conjunction with a female partner, and has this to say about the role of the man and the woman in the operation:

The alchemist and his 'mystical sister' collect the special dew together which will aid the life forces of their work. (From J.J. Mangetus, Bibliotheca Chemica Curiosa, *1702.)*

Through her extreme sensibility and the mobility of her own bodily fluids, the woman is to a certain extent in a favourable position to cross to higher levels and so receive instructions for her partner. His role, on the other hand, is far more earth-bound. He constructs the work on the material plane, at which level the woman stays in the background. She stands, therefore, on the right-hand side of the arcana, the 'passive side', the side of the psyche.

(Barbault 1975)

Sometimes it is implied that while the man may experiment and labour over his retorts and materials, the woman is needed to add the right touch to bring the work to life. There is an example of this in an early Chinese text:

A gentleman of the Yellow Gate at the Han [imperial court], Cheng Wei, loved the art of the Yellow and White [alchemy]. He took a wife and secured a girl from a household which knew recipes... [he tried to]

Male and female alchemists working together correspond to the key concepts of the alchemical pair of Sun and Moon, or gold and silver, interacting in the alchemical process. (Emblem 30, Michael Maier, Atlanta Fugiens, 1617.)

make gold in accordance with 'The Great Treasure' in the pillow [of the King of Huainan, but] it would not come. His wife however came and watched... Wei was then fanning the ashes to heat the bottle. In the bottle there was quicksilver. His wife said, 'I want to try and show you something.' She thereupon took a drug out of a bag and threw a very little into [the retort]. It was absorbed and in a short while she turned out [the contents of the retort]. It had already become silver. Wei was greatly astonished and said, 'The way of [alchemy] was near and was possessed by you. But why did you not tell me sooner?' His wife replied, 'In order to get it, it is necessary for one to have the [proper] fate'.

(Quoted in Taylor 1976: 67)

Both Helvetius, whom we shall meet towards the end of this chapter, and Nicolas Flamel worked in close collaboration with their wives. In the case of Helvetius, his wife spurred him on to experiment with the powdered stone he had been given when he himself despaired of any success in the matter: 'Late that night my wife (who was a most curious student and enquirer after the art) came soliciting and vexing me to make experiment of that little spark... saying to me, unless this be done, I shall have no rest nor sleep all this night.' Flamel, throughout the long years of his search, was dependent upon the help and encouragement of his wife Perenelle. Together they performed the perfect alchemical transmutation, and Flamel was more than ready to acknowledge Perenelle's essential contribution: 'I may speak it with truth, I have made it three times, with the help of Perenelle, who understood it as well as I because she helped me with my operations, and without doubt, if she would have enterprised to have done it alone, she had attained the end and perfection thereof.' (Flamel 1624)

Although alchemy was practised primarily by men, it was not forbidden in any way to women, and probably there were many women alchemists whose endeavours have passed unrecorded in history.

Laboratories and their inhabitants: mistakes and disasters

Contemporary paintings often show the laboratory as a busy place and one may be surprised to see a number of workers stoking, pounding, and pouring. Not all alchemists worked this way; in fact, using assistants is in some ways contrary to the spirit of alchemy, which demands secrecy and the total involvement of the practitioner rather than the delegation of work. However, the practical demands of a temperamental furnace needing to be kept at constant heat and of pots that must be watched lest they boil made the keeping of servants necessary for many. Thomas Norton decreed that eight in all would be ideal, but those of lesser fortunes might manage with four – two on duty and two that 'sleepeth or goeth to Kerke'. He also recommended that the alchemist should consult his own horoscope, especially the sixth house, to see how best to manage his servants.

The athanor (furnace) seems to have been free-standing, brick built, and about three feet in height with a conical cover on the top that could be taken off to allow a vessel to be placed in the chamber above the fire itself. Because pottery and glass vessels were needed, one of the great problems was breakages, especially at high temperatures. Thomas Charnock discusses the difficulties of ordering vessels, and of making the design explicit to the potter or the glassmaker without letting him know that it is intended for alchemical use. He advises telling the potter that the wares are needed to distil water to treat blindness; making the tabernacle (or support for the vessel) needs the co-operation of a joiner, who can be told that it is a burrow for a fox!

Charnock had first-hand experience of laboratory catastrophe:

> Yet one thing of truth I weill thee tell,
> What greate mishap unto my worke befell;
> It was upon a New Yeare's Day at noon,
> My tabernacle caught fire, it was soon done:
> For within an hour it was right well,
> And straight of fire I had a smell. I ran up to my work right,
> And when I came it was on a fire light:
> Then was I in such fear that I began to stagger,
> As if I had been wounded to the heart with a dagger;
> And can you blame me? no I think not much,
> For if I had been a man anything rich,
> I had rather have given 100 Marks to the Poor,
> Rather than that hap should have chanced that hour.
> For I was well onward of my work truly.

(*The Breviary of Philosophy* in Ashmole 1652: 293)

Explosions and poisonings being well-known hazards of the alchemical laboratory, it is little wonder that the alchemical quest was thought of as a dangerous one, and the constant effort and devotion alchemy demanded could easily turn to obsessive mania. Bernard of Treves and Godfrey Leporis (also fourteenth century), for instance, spent ten years in unsuccessful experiment, using over 2,000 hens' eggs in one project. Bernard desisted only when he was rendered unconscious by the fumes of vitriol for fourteen months. When he recovered he sold all his estate to pay his debts, and then took up alchemy again.

Some texts, such as *The Sophic Hydrolith,* give guidance so that the alchemist may judge when matters are not progressing satisfactorily. Premature redness, lack of coagulation and so on are 'symptoms of a false composition and temperature, or of some kind or other of carelessness'. The author continues: 'If these defects are not immediately seen to, they will speedily become incorrigible. A cunning adept should be acquainted with the various devices by which they may be remedied; and I will recount them here for the sake of the beginner... ' A far worse fate is promised by an early Chinese writer should the student go astray:

> Gases from food consumed will make noises inside the intestines and stomach. The right essence will be exhaled and the evil one inhaled. Days and nights will be passed without sleep, moon after moon. The body will then be tired out, giving rise to an appearance of insanity. The hundred pulses will stir and boil so violently as to drive away peace of mind and body... Ghostly things will make their appearance, at which he will marvel even in his sleep. He is then led to rejoice, thinking that he is assured of longevity. But all of a sudden he is seized by an untimely death.

> (Wei Po-yang [second century AD] quoted in Jung 1967)

Letting the world at large know that you practised alchemy could be dangerous: if people associated alchemy with the devil, they might hang you; if they thought you possessed a secret for making gold they would pursue you greedily: with kings and potentates, it was often a case of 'prove it or die'. Sometimes laws were passed forbidding the practice of alchemy, or else insisting that a special licence be obtained if the alchemist could prove himself to be a genuine seeker. The author of *An Open Entrance to the Closed Palace of the King* paints a most pathetic picture of the alchemists' lot:

> So long as the secret is possessed by a comparatively small number of philosophers, their lot is anything but a bright and happy one; surrounded as we are on every side by the cruel greed and the prying suspicion of the multitude, we are doomed, like Cain, to wander over the earth homeless and friendless. Not for us are the soothing influences of domestic happiness; not for us the delightful confidences of friendship. Men who covet

Alchemical assistants working under the direction of their master. (From MS of Elias Ashmole, Theatrum Chemicum Britannicum, *seventeenth century, opp. p45, The Bodleian Library, University of Oxford.)*

our golden secret pursue us from place to place, and fear closes our lips, when love tempts us to open ourselves freely to a brother. Thus we feel prompted at times to burst forth into the desolate exclamation of Cain: 'Whoever finds me will slay me.' Yet we are not the murderers of our brethren; we are anxious only to do good to our fellow-men. But even our kindness and charitable compassion are rewarded with black ingratitude – ingratitude that cries to heaven for vengeance. It was only a short time ago that, after visiting the plague-stricken haunts of a certain city, and restoring the sick to perfect health by means of my miraculous medicine, I found myself surrounded by a yelling mob, who demanded that I should give to them my Elixir of the Sages; and it was only by changing my dress and my name, by shaving off my beard and putting on a wig, that I was enabled to save my life...

Anon, attributed to Eirenaes Philalethes (in Waite 1893).

Learning and teaching

> All hail to the noble company
> Of true students in holy alchemy,
> Whose noble practice does them teach
> To veil their secrets with misty speech...

The Hunting of the Green Lion (anon) (in Ashmole 1652: 278)

Some kindly advice to the alchemical novice is given in another of Philalethes' treatises as follows:In the first place, let him carry on his operations with great secrecy in order that no scornful or scurrilous person may know of them; for nothing discourages the beginner so much as the mockery, taunts and well-meant advice of foolish outsiders. Moreover, if he does not succeed, secrecy will save him from derision; if he does succeed, it will safeguard him against the persecution of greedy and cruel tyrants. In the second place, he who would succeed in the study of this Art should be persevering, industrious, learned, gentle, good-tempered, a close student, and neither easily discouraged nor slothful; he may work in co-operation with one friend, not more, but should be able to keep his own counsel; it is also necessary that he should have a little capital to procure the necessary implements, etc, and to provide himself with food and clothing while he follows this study, so that his mind may be undistracted by care and anxiety. Above all, let him be honest, God-fearing, prayerful and holy. Being thus equipped, he should study Nature, read the books of the genuine Sages, who are neither imposters nor jealous churls, and study them day and night...

(From *The Treatises of Philalethes* in Waite 1893)

Many would-be alchemists tried to learn the secrets of the art through books and manuscripts available to them. These could produce an alternating frenzy of hope and despair as work after work was studied and then cast aside with the riddle still unsolved.

One frank account comes from Denis Zachaire, a French alchemist of the sixteenth century:

There [in Paris in 1546] for 10 crowns I bought books of philosophy, ancient as well as modern, part of which were printed while others were written by hand... And having hired for myself a small room in the Faubourg Saint-Marceau, I lived there for a year, with a small boy who served me, without frequenting anyone, studying day and night on those authors, with the result that at the end of the month I made one conclusion, and then another, then I changed it almost entirely. So, while waiting for a conclusion in which there was not variety nor contradiction between the sentences of the books of the philosophers, I spent an entire year and part of another without being able to gain over my study to the extent of being able to make any entire and perfect conclusion.

(Quoted in Holmyard 1957)

It was the convention in alchemical writing for each author to slip in a hint that no work had ever been so bold, so explicit, so ready to give away cherished secrets.

This was usually followed by a condemnation of all the wicked lies that had been passed off as alchemical truths in other books:

When I considered in my mind the great number of deceitful books and forged Alchemistic 'receipts', which have been put into circulation by heartless imposters, though they do not contain even a spark of truth – and how many persons have been and are still daily led astray by them? – it occurred to me that I could not do better than communicate the Talent committed to me by the Father of Light to the Sons and Heirs of Knowledge.

(Michael Sendivogius, *The New Chemical Light,* in Waite 1893)

Often the reader is lured on with promises of frank revelations. But time and time again this is not to be; the author slips in an apology for not going any further, but indicates that he has already said more than he should, 'But if the complement is concealed let not the son of learning wonder. For we have not concealed it from him, but have delivered it in such a speech, as it must necessarily be hid from the evil, and unjust, and the unwise cannot discern it.' (Pseudo-Geber, *The Sum of Perfection*)

The message of the written texts seems to be: Let those who understand already understand what I have written; let those who are ignorant remain ignorant.

Although some students claimed to have mastered alchemical practice through books, most needed a more direct contact with the tradition. Over and over again alchemists emphasise the fact that if the mystery is not revealed directly through a dream or vision, then it must come from 'living Masters'. Thomas Norton tells us that 'it must needs be taught from mouth to mouth', and that not even one's own children are entitled to learn it. He himself says that his master (George Ripley) tested his sincerity in various ways, one of which was by requiring him to ride a hundred miles in each direction to spend a forty-day training period with his teacher. Students are advised against wasting their money on tuition from any vain boaster who claims to be skilled in alchemy. Only those who know nothing, it is said, talk freely. If you are offered instruction:

> Spend not thy money away in waste,
> Give not to every speech credence;
> But first examine, grope and taste;
> And as thou provest, so put thy confidence,
> And ever beware of great expense...
> One thing, one glass, one furnace and no more,
> Behold this principle if he take,
> And if he do not, then let him go...

(Ripley 1591, in Ashmole 1652)

Some of the stories concerning the initiation of alchemists are fascinating, but even apparently factual narratives may be to some extent allegorical. Historians are generally pleased to quote the testimony of **Helvetius** (Johann Friedrich Schweitzer), for this appears to be a straightforward account of a meeting between Helvetius and an alchemical adept. The story is recounted in *The Golden Calf*, and tells how on 27 December 1666 a stranger appeared at Helvetius' house in The Hague, and showed him some pieces of matter 'each about the bigness of a small walnut, transparent, of a pale brimstone colour', which the stranger said was the Philosopher's Stone. He refused to give Helvetius any of it, but talked to him about how he could turn stones into gems, produce healing medicines, and make 'a limpid clear water sweeter than honey' (probably the famed Mercurial water). He showed

An alchemist reading; studying the enigmatic writings of other alchemists was considered an essential part of the quest. (From a German alchemical poem, seventeenth century MS. Add. A. 287, p9, Bodleian Library.)

Helvetius some golden medals that had been struck from alchemical gold. Three weeks later, he returned, and after much pleading from Helvetius, gave him a tiny 'crumb' of the stone. When Helvetius doubted that such a small amount could do anything at all, the stranger took it back, threw half of it into the fire, and gave him back the rest. He instructed him in the art of preparing the stone, telling him that only two substances in all are necessary, and that the work is carried out in one crucible and is neither lengthy nor expensive if correctly understood. He did not return again, but Helvetius, with the assistance of his wife, performed a successful transmutation with the stone, and the gold which was produced was publicly assayed and found to be of excellent quality.

Some scholars have found this story difficult to assess, for on the one hand Helvetius was a respected physician and botanical writer, not given to deliberate deception; yet on the other, the tale of marvellous gold produced in this way seems to them to have little credibility. I would suggest that much of the tale is likely to be allegory.

A clever man such as Helvetius is quite capable of weaving his knowledge of alchemical training into a kind of parable, which contains much information and truth but not in a literal fashion.

Indeed, it is much more likely that he would do this than that he would openly describe his training, since it was normal for this to be kept secret.

The stranger who mysteriously arrives is described as wearing 'a plebeian habit, honest Gravity, and serious authority; of a mean stature, a little long face, with a few small pock holes, and most black hair, not at all curled, a beardless chin, about three or four and forty years of age (as I guessed)'. Such a description is a perfect portrait of Saturn personified. The astrological attributes of Saturn (as we have seen, alchemists were well-versed in planetary lore) when applied to human appearance are leanness, dark hair and complexion, a lowliness of clothing and height, and a serious manner. Saturn, additionally was sometimes depicted as the wise guide and instructor in alchemy, who could lead the initiate to understanding. Even the anecdotal detail that the stranger forgot to wipe the snow and mud off his boots when entering Helvetius' nicely-furnished room has a significance in this context, for Saturn is the planet of dirt and earth, and those under his influence are said to be somewhat grubby in their own manners and appearance.

And what of Helvetius himself, as he portrays his reactions? His behaviour is just like that of Mercury, the agent of alchemy – ever-questioning, arguing, even trying to steal the Stone at one point. Mercury is the natural active force of alchemy; in its primal state it is volatile and unreliable and must be disturbed, released and then fixed in a higher state in order to bring about the transformation.

Nicolas Flamel, who lived in the fourteenth century, leaves us another account of discovering alchemy. This may perhaps be a more straightforward narrative, but we cannot be certain. Flamel, a notary living in Paris, dreamed of a wonderfully illustrated book, which he later actually came across and purchased. It seemed to be made out of 'delicate rinds... Of tender young trees.' It was covered in brass and inscribed with strange characters; it contains twenty-one leaves and was 'full of fair figures', such as Mercury, a virgin swallowed by serpents, a crucified serpent (the slain mercury that has to be resurrected), and a mountain with her 'fair flower' on the top (probably the metallic seed of the First Substance). Flamel and his wife Perenelle, whom he had lately married in middle age, pored over this together, after he had spent many solitary hours trying to unravel it secrets. Although she could not understand it any better than he, Flamel found it a great comfort to study it with her. He had the emblems painted in

A teacher initiates his pupil into the mysteries of alchemy: 'Receive the gift of God under the sacred rule.' 'I will keep the mysteries of alchemy secretly.' (From MS Ashmole 971, Theatrum Chemicum Britannicum, seventeenth century, p14, The Bodleian Library, University of Oxford.)

his house, and he consulted some of the ' greatest clerks' in Paris as to their meaning. He understood that they were to do with the making of the Stone, but he could not get far with his interpretation of them. At last, frustrated by twenty-one years of study and experimentation, Flamel left the country in a pilgrim's habit to seek elucidation of the book overseas.

In Leon, in Spain, he was directed to a Jewish merchant who was known to be 'very skilful in sublime sciences'. This Master Canches was overjoyed to see copies of the figures that Flamel had brought with him and implied that they were from a most important text which had been thought lost. He and Flamel returned to France together so that Canches could translate and decipher the whole of the book. Canches died before reaching Paris, but he had already given Flamel enough knowledge of the principles of alchemy for him to begin the process again in a different manner, and we are told that Nicolas and Perenelle finally made the Elixir together, which was immediately recognisable 'by the strong scent and odour thereof.' They performed the projection with the Elixir, and transmuted mercury into gold, a gold' better assuredly than common gold, more soft and pliable.' The story concludes by relating that they were able to give all the gold they made on this and later occasions to charity, to build hospitals and look after widows and orphans. Flamel certainly existed; his tombstone can still be seen, adorned with emblems of the Sun and Moon, in the Museum of Cluny. How much of his story is true we do not know; but like the testimony of Helvetius, it gives us a valuable insight into the nature of the alchemical quest. Emphasis is given in the narrative to the persistence and devotion of Flamel, to the need for him to work in ignorance for many years until he came, through destiny or luck, to meet the right teacher. His quest, like many others, was a mixture of personal effort and inspired guidance, needing half a lifetime to reach perfection.

Chapter Five

A mirror of the world

Does such a secretive, enigmatic study as alchemy have any relevance at all to the world at large? How could it possibly benefit humanity, or add to our general store of knowledge, especially when its adherents make a virtue out of keeping its inner teachings strictly to themselves? However any philosophy, religious movement or esoteric study can serve as a ground plan for human endeavour if it there is truth at its heart. If its structure is rooted in universal principles, in what is sometimes referred to as 'the perennial philosophy', then it can affect every level of human existence, right through from the spiritual to the practical. Even if its inner teachings remain concealed, perhaps for a number of years, perhaps permanently, it will almost inevitably affect the course of human endeavour sooner or later. Esoteric becomes exoteric; theory turns into practice; abstract becomes concrete. The capacity of a wisdom tradition to bear fruit in everyday life in such ways is at least as important as the illumination of its followers.

The everyday influence of alchemy can be traced in scientific discoveries, in literature and the arts, and in the development of modern psychology. Sometimes these developments were brought about by those who were themselves deeply involved in the study of alchemy; sometimes they were the result of borrowings from the alchemical framework and language. Some discoveries, particularly in the scientific field, were by-products of working on the alchemical process, whereas other applications of alchemy were fuelled by taking the essence of its philosophy and symbolism and creating afresh.

This chapter and the two that follow explore how alchemy served as inspiration in different contexts. In certain cases the link is very direct, in others it may be speculative, or be tied in to other occult and philosophical traditions. Points at which such traditions, especially ones as secretive as alchemy, cross the threshold into the outer world are not always easy to spot. Discovering such points, however, can be tremendously exciting, reconnecting us with the energy of the original inspiration, and broadening and enlivening our vision of the subject concerned. Perhaps it is not too fanciful to say that such recognition is the completion of the creative process: the spiritual impulse works its way through to a material form; the impulse is forgotten; then, when it is rediscovered, by people from a different time and place, it rebinds itself to the divine creative force ('religion' means 'to rebind') making a new link between the temporal and the eternal. This in its turn can lead to further creation, just as the reconnection with the philosophy of the ancient masters Plato and Aristotle, and with the hermetic texts, helped to inspire the European Renaissance – the word 'Renaissance' itself means 'rebirth'.

Inevitably, as knowledge is brought into the general realm, it can become dissipated, and even undermine existing spiritual traditions. Isaac Newton, as we shall see in the following chapter, was both a passionate mystic and an alchemical adept, and yet his scientific discoveries led to a school of scientific thought that rejected anything that could not be weighed, measured or quantified. Dion Fortune, an occult writer associated with the Golden Dawn (see Chapter Eight) and other esoteric orders, remarked darkly that techniques commonly used by advertising agencies were once only known to initiates of such orders. In this case, one may surmise that such techniques, probably involving the power of image and suggestion, may not only have become popularised but have also been applied to very dubious ends. Such examples make more sense of the anxiety of the alchemists to keep their knowledge hidden, lest it should fall into the wrong hands.

Alchemy and baroque music

This exploration begins, as the Lady Alchymia steps out shyly into the sunlight, with a look at the link between alchemy and the birth of baroque music. These two subjects have rarely been linked, and yet there is a powerful connection between them. The greatest composer of the time, Claudio Monteverdi, was a practising alchemist, and other leading composers of the day were dedicated to tapping sources of ancient wisdom and channelling it into their work; studies of this kind prevalent in northern Italy at the time included alchemy, Neoplatonism, astrology, and the Kabbalah.

Baroque music, as this 'new music' came to be known, arose in the years between 1570 and 1610. Its effect was remarkable, for in that brief period, music was revolutionised. New forms of solo singing and

Wall painting from San Gimignano, Italy, in a series of images which appear to represent the alchemical process: this is the marriage of male and female, sun and moon.

instrumental music were created; music and drama found a true fusion, and from their union sprang opera and oratorio. Its innovation heralded a musical era which lasted for nearly two hundred years, and whose composers included such great names as Bach, Handel, Purcell and Vivaldi. Many of its forms and idioms have remained in musical currency until the present day, and of course baroque music itself is alive and well on the concert platform. Indeed, the music is appreciated more than ever before – there is a growing love of its clarity and beauty, of music which is structured as graciously as fine architecture, yet is also full of vitality and power.

When we start digging down to discover the connections between alchemy and baroque music, we come across different kinds of evidence. There are direct links: Monteverdi's recorded interest in alchemy, and his avowed intent to weave philosophical truths into his music. There are inferences to be made: from the fact that alchemical practice was widespread in northern Italy at the time, and that the groups of learned men and composers working to create a new form of music would have almost certainly included it among their mystical and metaphysical studies. Finally, there are the parallels which we ourselves can spot between the practice of alchemy and baroque

In another fresco from San Gimignano, the royal pair are 'washed' in the bath, a standard stage of the alchemical process to remove impurities and prepare the way for transformation.

music, all leading to a greater understanding of the creative process at work behind the compositions.

We are just at the beginning of this fascinating exploration, and I think it likely that more and more evidence connecting the two subjects will be brought to light in future years. In later chapters I offer you examples of other links already researched between alchemy and the arts and sciences; in this chapter I present my own area of investigation, which has captured my attention both as a singer specialising in this period of music, and as a writer focusing on 'magical philosophies' such as alchemy.

Monteverdi, alchemy and the Florentine Camerata

There was a strong tradition of alchemical study in northern Italy, which was composed geographically of various independent ducal states. Many dukes and nobles showed a keen interest in alchemy, in a climate of learning that was favourable to occult traditions set in a framework of studies which covered a wide spectrum of arts and natural sciences. Often the traces of alchemical study remain in the buildings themselves. A room was set aside in the Uffizi Palace in Florence for the study of alchemy, and apparently the 'studiolo' or

This final example from San Gimignano, a bedroom scene, probably represents the 'coniunctio' or mating of the alchemical couple.

small study in the Palazzo Vecchio, also in Florence, was dedicated to the same purpose. Both these would have been used in the sixteenth century. Dating from an earlier period, alchemical paintings can be found in the Palazzo del Popolo in San Gimignano, near Siena. These frescoes are thought to have been painted by Memmo di Filipuccio between 1303 and 1317. Those that survive cover a large part of the walls of a small upper room in the tower (one of the famous medieval 'skyscraper' towers of the city) and depict themes such as the wedding and bedding of the alchemical King and Queen, the immersion of the royal pair in the bath, and the flagellation of the man/animal representing the First Substance. A six-petalled golden flower, symbolising the alchemical goal, is repeated as a motif over the frescoes, and a mysterious lady, probably the Lady Alchymia herself, as the spirit of alchemy was often represented, acts as guide and initiator into each new pictorial sequence. Strangely enough, these have not yet been recognised by scholars as alchemical, although near exact illustrative parallels can be found in many alchemical sources; one guidebook assumes that they represent 'an evident moralizing intention... showing what dangers one can meet with in succumbing to female seduction.'

The Gonzaga Palace in Mantua, northern Italy, where Monteverdi almost certainly learnt alchemy at the ducal court.

Returning to the sixteenth century, Vincenzo Gonzaga, the Duke of Mantua, and Monteverdi's first patron, was a keen student of alchemy and he was probably the key figure who initiated the young composer into the art. Monteverdi's own practice of alchemy lasted a lifetime, and a sonnet written in his praise shortly after his death described him as a 'Great Master of Alchemy'. There are various mentions of alchemy in Monteverdi's letters, although he is, in the best tradition, cryptic in his references. He describes and draws a vessel for calcinating gold with lead, and speaks of his own experiments in making mercury from 'unrefined matter which changes into clear water' which, 'although it will be in water it will not however lose its identity as mercury, or its weight.' In later letters he conceals the nature of substances he is referring to, speaking only of 'a pot of it,' 'a small jar of it' and 'a certain something.'

These letters were written during Monteverdi's later years when he worked as master of music at St Mark's Basilica, Venice, and composed some of his finest works, such as the *Vespers* of 1610. The editor of his letters refers to Gonzaga's interest in alchemy as 'an unhealthy enthusiasm for the pseudo-sciences' and suggests that Monteverdi's own involvement 'could not have been all that deep'

An alchemist's laboratory, with musical instruments in the foreground. (From Heinrich Khunrath Amphitheatre of Eternal Wisdom, *1609)*

(Stevens 1980). And yet it is widely accepted that Monteverdi was ardently involved with the quest for wisdom, a follower of Plato actively endeavouring to centre his music around those truths. 'My intention is to show by means of our practice [i.e. musical practice, his 'Seconda Pratica'] what I have been able to extract from the mind of those philosophers for the benefit of good art.' We shall consider some of those means later. For the moment, I would simply like to suggest that alchemy, a subject in which Monteverdi undeniably took a great interest, and for which he became famous as an adept, surely influenced his musical composition just as his study of the classical philosophers did.

St Mark's Basilica, Venice, where Monteverdi channelled his alchemical interest into the music he wrote for the choir and musicians.

Indeed, music was considered an intrinsic part of alchemy by many alchemists of the period. Sometimes the Great Work was conducted with the assistance of musical chants. Illustrations contemporary with the beginnings of baroque music such as those contained in *Splendor Solis*, by Trismosin (*circa* 1582) and *The Amphitheatre of Eternal Wisdom* by Heinrich Khunrath (1609) show musical instruments in the laboratory, or groups of players and singers as emblematic of stages in the alchemical process. Music could be a magical aid in the laboratory, invoking, perhaps, planetary spirits; it was also a guide to cosmic laws in which the power of vibration, sound and mathematical ratios may be understood.

An even more fascinating and direct use of music in alchemy is found in Michael Maier's *Atlanta Fugiens* (1617). Here Maier sets fifty vocal fugues for three voices as musical illustrations for the beautifully drawn alchemical emblems, many of which are well known in their own right. They are more than illustrations: they are, Maier says, 'for the soul's recreation... to be looked at, read, meditated, understood, weighed, sung and listened to, not without a certain pleasure.' Music and alchemy had already found their fusion in the alchemical laboratory; while Maier cultivated this connection within the hermetic sphere, composers such as Monteverdi took it out into the wider cultural field.

Monteverdi was an individualist; although he took note of progress made by other composers in the field, he felt that he had to work out his own salvation, with the help of such traditions as Neoplatonism and alchemy. However, the earliest developments of baroque music in the late sixteenth century were inspired by collective study. The group responsible is generally known as 'the Florentine Camerata', an active fraternity of musicians, scholars and nobles, whose avowed aim was to restore music to the glory of ancient classical civilisation, with the help not only of the philosophers of the time but of a whole range of metaphysical, mystical and magical studies, in which alchemy would have found a natural place. The key figure in organising the groups which met was Giovanni Bardi, whose son later wrote:

> My father, Signor Giovanni, who took great delight in
> music and was in his day a composer of some
> reputation, always had about him the most celebrated
> men of the city, learned in this profession, and inviting
> them to his house, he formed a sort of delightful and
> continual academy, from which vice and in particular
> every kind of gaming were absent. To this the noble
> youth of Florence were attracted with great profit to
> themselves, passing their time not only in pursuit of
> music, but also in discussing and receiving instruction
> in poetry, astrology and other sciences which by turns
> lent value to this pleasant converse.

(Strunk 1981)

The Florentine Camerata was an academy (in fact it probably consisted of two or three consecutive groups) following a tradition established in Florence in 1459 by Marsilio Ficino. Ficino responded to a request from the reigning duke, Cosimo di Medici, to found a new school of study based on the rediscovered writings of Plato and the Hermetic texts (see page 116). Here, studies in Kabbalah and astrology interwove with these classical and hermetic themes, and its members endeavoured to show that there was no fundamental clash between such teachings and Christianity. This original Florentine Academy had a profound effect upon the religious and artistic outlook of the time. It was succeeded by a number of other academies, each with a slightly different outlook or intention.

The Florentine Camerata, over one hundred years later, maintained this broad outlook, but applied it to specific musical goals. Its output was at first rather pedantic; making music by committee resulted, not unsurprisingly, in somewhat contrived compositions. However, certain principles that its members laid down began to bear fruit; the declamatory style (later known as 'recitative') was devised from their interpretation of Greek drama, giving a means of turning the passionate expression of speech into music. Soon true individual creativity started to reveal itself with composers such as Giulio Caccini and Jacopo Peri whose work has proved to be of lasting value. In keeping with the traditions of wisdom they turned to for inspiration, their goals were spiritual ones: Caccini wrote that the aim of music was to appear as 'a pattern and true resemblance of those never ceasing celestial harmonies whence proceed so many good effects and benefits upon earth, raising and exciting the minds of the hearers to the contemplation of those infinite delights which Heaven affordeth.' (Caccini, *Le nuove musiche 1602*, quoted in Strunk 1981)

In general terms, such aims paralleled those of alchemy. As with alchemical practice, members of the Camerata also believed that humans can actively participate in the creative process in the universe, that we are not passive onlookers but can weave our own magic, and invoke presences of gods and angels. The gods, it was said, can be affected by our music. Antecedents for this are found in the writings of Ficino who recommended using music as a means to call down the planetary deities. (Yates 1954: 77–8) This is turn derives from Orphic practices, which are linked in time and context with the hermetic writings (see page 116), bringing us back full circle to alchemy. The prevalent hermetic interest in Italy in the Renaissance can also be judged from the marble pavement in the Cathedral in Siena, where striking portraits of Hermes Trismegistus (see page 37) and the ten prophetic Sibyls can be seen.

Nature and music

> Let Nature be your guide, and with your art
> Follow her closely. Without her you'll err.
> Let reason be your staff; experience lend

Power to your sight, that you may see afar.
Let reading be your lamp, dispelling dark,
That you may guard 'gainst throngs of things and words.

(Epigram 42 – Michael Maier – *Atlanta Fugiens*)

Let us turn now to examine more specific alchemical ideas as they appear in baroque music. Some may be culled directly from the alchemical tradition, whereas others may have been derived from a synthesis of alchemy, astrology, kabbalism and Neoplatonism. There are in any case many parallels and overlaps between those traditions, which constantly borrowed one from the other. We are standing on one of those elusive thresholds, the point at which esoteric becomes exoteric, tentatively remaking that connection so that our understanding and appreciation of music can be re-energised.

First of all, alchemy and baroque music emphasise the role of Nature, as a guiding principle, as a teacher whose ways were to be understood, imitated, and transformed through art. The word 'natural' occurs time and time again in the writings of the Florentine Camerata. The members felt that artifice had taken the place of a natural approach to music. They aimed to create a music that would sound natural and spontaneous and yet be of great subtlety, with the power to move the listener and evoke the 'heavenly harmonies' within an earthly framework. The human voice was their touchstone of the natural and instinctive, the 'Primal Material' of musical alchemy. In practical terms this resulted in an emphasis on a solo voice, where words and expression might be properly communicated, on the avoidance of extremes in pitch and dynamic – the singer, said Caccini, should 'so pitch his tune as to sing in his clear and natural voice' – and the addition of ornaments only where they served to grace the music, rather than to show off the performer's expertise.

A quotation from the famous illuminated alchemical manuscript *Splendor Solis* echoes this approach:

> Art goes quite another way to work, with different
> intention from Nature, therefore does Art also use
> different tools and instruments. For that reason can Art
> produce extraordinary things out of the aforesaid natural
> beginnings such as Nature of herself would not be able
> to create.

(*Splendor Solis* 1582)

Monteverdi also pays tribute to the importance of seeking out the natural and transforming it into music of great power and refinement. Like the alchemists, he believed in searching the wisdom of the ancient masters for clues but then working out one's own solution. In a letter written in 1633, Monteverdi says that he sought 'a natural way of imitation,' but that when he was composing his *Lament of Arianna* (one of his most famous and profound pieces) 'no book could show me... not even one that would explain how I ought to become an imitator... I found out (let me tell you) what hard work I had to do in order to achieve the little I did do in the way of imitation.' However, in a subsequent letter written in February 1634, he acknowledges that he had found a certain guidance from 'the principles of the best philosophers to have investigated nature.' (Stevens 1980)

Searching the ancient wisdom, the forgotten knowledge and despised material, working intensively from one's own observations, often until near breaking point, was the way in which both the alchemist and the baroque composer struggled to release the potent forces of Nature and begin the process of creation. In his account of the Florentine Camerata, Pietro de' Bardi recalls how his father, in collaboration with Vincenzo Galilei, a founding member and father of the famous astronomer Galileo Galilei, dedicated himself to the quest:

> This great intellect [Galilei] recognised that, besides restoring ancient music... one of the chief aims of the academy was to improve modern music... Thus he was the first to let us hear singing in *stile rappresentativo*, in which arduous undertaking, then considered almost ridiculous, he was chiefly encouraged and assisted by my father, who toiled for entire nights and incurred great expense for the sake of this noble discovery.

> (Strunk 1981)

The composers who 'invented' baroque music – the Florentine Camerata, Monteverdi and his contemporaries – did not simply feel a song coming on and write it down. Like the alchemists, they worked with conscious intent, using a combination of the ancient wisdom, personal repeated effort, observation and individual vision to achieve the transformation.

Battling duos, harmonious trios

The next parallel between music and alchemy can be found in the generation of warring opposites. One of the radical innovations in

'*For him versed in Chemistry, let Nature, Reason,
Experience, and Reading be his Guide, staff, spectacles and
lamp.*' *(Emblem 42, Michael Maier,* Atlanta Fugiens, *1617.)*

baroque music was that it deliberately employed the use of sharp
successive contrasts, to increase tension and heighten the drama of a
piece. Often these contrasts are quite violent, and occur within a very
short musical space, so that, for instance, within a sacred choral piece
one may hear the voices join in a few bars of smooth polyphony, and
then break into an urgent, agitated passage. At the time this must have
been almost shocking, but very exciting. In alchemy, early in the
process, the First Matter is violently split into two to release the
dynamic polarities within. The stage is often described as a battle, a
duel between a pair of men, dogs or dragons. This energy can then be
used to fuel the alchemical transformation; in order to arrive at final
resolution and transformation, conflict must be provoked. 'I was aware
that it is contraries that greatly move our mind, and... this is the
purpose which all good music should have' Monteverdi wrote, as he

described his search to find a form of music fitting to represent warfare – a search to which he 'applied [himself] with no small diligence and toil.' (Foreword to *Madrigali Guerrieri ed Amorosi [Madrigals of War and Love]* quoted in Strunk 1981.)

This leads to our next correspondence, moving from the concept of a basic duality to that of the three forces which may be seen to underpin both the alchemical process and a musical structure. In music they correspond to three 'modes' of expression; in alchemy they are salt, mercury and sulphur, or body, soul and spirit. This fundamental triplicity is not exclusive to alchemy, and is found with different names in the Kabbalah, in Platonic philosophy and of course in the Christian doctrine of the Trinity. However, actively working with the triplicity, rather than just acknowledging it, is especially emphasised in alchemy, and this process of engaging with the three forces may, I believe, give us insight into the interpretation of Baroque music.

It was Monteverdi who innovated and established this principle of a threefold means of expression in music.

> I have reflected that the principal passions or affections
> of our mind are three, namely, anger, moderation, and
> humility or supplication; so the best philosophers
> declare, and the very nature of our voice indicates this
> in having high, low and middle registers. The art of
> music also points to these three in its terms 'agitated',
> 'soft' and 'moderate' (*concitato, molle* and *temperato*).
> In all the works of former composers I have indeed
> found examples of the 'soft' and the 'moderate', but
> never of the 'agitated'.

> (Quoted in Strunk 1981)

Thus Monteverdi began work on creating a means of musically representing warfare, as mentioned above. Basically, the style he evolved, known as *'concitato'*, consists of rapidly reiterated notes which are centred on a regular pulse but adapted to the rhythm and sense of the words being sung.

Possibly this dynamic working trinity may underlie musical composition of the time to a greater extent than has hitherto been realised. With his Platonic and alchemical training, Monteverdi would have seen the triplicity not simply as a trio of emotions demanding expression, but as a way of describing the fundamental three forces of

A volume of Monteverdi's music preserved in the church where he is buried in Venice, the Chiesa Dei Frari.

creation in human terms. Michael Maier, in his alchemical fugues, did just that, using the classical myth of Atlanta, the swift-footed virgin, and personifying mercury, sulphur and salt as Atlanta, Hippomenes and the Golden Apple respectively. Here the three voices sing concurrently; their parts are structured to symbolise their individual natures, and the harmonies and musical progressions symbolise the changing interaction between them. Both Maier's own preface to the work and editorial analysis leave no doubt that he intended to paint as dynamic a musical portrait of the alchemical triplicity as possible, turning the philosophic mercury, the fiery sulphur and the quiet, steady salt into living music.

So far, we have seen that the three creative forces of alchemy can be musically structured both in terms of harmony and also as stylistic modes of expression. Furthermore, they may have been used to provide a sectional ground plan for music, in which each part of the triplicity is highlighted in turn. If we look at certain compositions in this light, new avenues of interpretation open up. For example, we can find evidence of this in Monteverdi's extended solo lament *Lamento d'Arianna*, written in 1608, This was originally the climactic piece of a complete opera based on the myth of Ariadne and Theseus, considered a masterpiece in its day but now unfortunately lost in its entirety. The lament is a complex succession of emotions as Ariadne faces her abandonment, and her mixed passions of love and anger for Theseus. However, if we consider it as falling into three sections, immediately the predominating mood of each reveals itself in accord with the 'molle', the 'concitato' and the 'moderato'. In the first section, Ariadne alternately begs for death and for Theseus to return to her; it is the 'molle', the soft, beseeching, loving force. In the second, her resentment and anger takes over; she invokes tempests and whirlwinds to destroy Theseus on his journey home. Here, plainly, is the 'concitato' style, both in theme and in musical notation. Finally, she enters the state of 'moderato'; her grief is still present, but she becomes reconciled with dignity to her fate, and takes farewell of her parents and her homeland. Her fate, she says, is of one who has loved and trusted too much.

Using this triplicity as a key to this marvellous, difficult and lengthy piece, provides a revelation of interpretation, a guide to the singer and listener. The triplicity also structures the lament as a complete miniature tragedy in its own right (it was considered to be such at the time) ending, through the *moderato* mode, with a kind of ultimate resolution and reconciliation.

The cosmic stage

The audience watching a baroque opera is like an alchemist gazing into his vessel. The changing fortunes of kings and queens, intimate visions of the gods and the interaction of heaven and earth are dramas which are witnessed by both. Just as the alchemist saw his vessel as a miniature cosmos, so the baroque stage was a complete world; it was even set out so that one part represented heaven and another earth. Certain stage plays of the period also exhibit alchemical overtones, and in Chapter Seven we can look more closely at these. Opera, however, was more cosmological; gods, angels, spirits and figures from allegories move among mortals in a way that is rarer in plays and there is a more obvious sense of magical evocation. Its music, as with Ficino's hymns, is used as a means to create communion between earthly and heavenly forces.

Opera was thus not merely a performance; by putting drama into music one was actually calling forth the spirit of the gods and that of the myth, which was usually taken from classical sources. Both opera

The grave of the composer Claudio Monteverdi in the Chiesa dei Frari, Venice.

and alchemy were seen as active, participatory processes – alchemy too used classical mythology at this time to describe the different stages of the work. In opera, music was the means to awaken the myth, and all – composer, performers and audience – were participants in the process.

Curiously enough, this notion of participation is expressed very plainly in the English masque form. Masques were glorious costumed displays of music, song and dance, given with dazzling effects of colour and lighting. Plots were thin or non-existent, but there was great emphasis on representing different levels of creation, so that angels and apes might take the stage together. Masques were almost always performed by and given before the nobility, ideally with the king and queen present. The cosmos was revealed, with the alchemical king and queen as witnesses. Then, at the end of the masque, the audience was obliged to get up and join in the dancing, with the king and queen, or highest ranking couple there, leading the festivities. There is no proof as yet that alchemy was a direct inspiration for this, but I think that alchemy explains very well just why the form of the masque should be structured this way.

In this chapter we have opened out the enclosed, secretive world of alchemy and looked at its influence on baroque music. By doing this, a door opens; more and more possibilities present themselves, and one begins to see that our understanding of music of the time could be profoundly affected by this knowledge. I would like to think that by understanding the relationship between alchemy and music, both factual and conceptual, we may find inspiration powerful enough to affect the course of future music composition and performance. It is more than a new light on old music; it could be the key to releasing new creativity and to transforming the present musical structures by which composers, performers and audiences are bound. Alchemy and music of the sixteenth and seventeenth centuries both had the same aim: 'Hermes, a Father of Philosophy, says: "It is indeed needed that at the End of this World, Heaven and Earth should meet and come home."' (*Splendor Solis*).

Chapter Six

Alchemy as a spiritual discipline

The greedy cheat with impure hands may not
Attempt this Art, nor is it ever got
By the unlearned and rude: the vicious mind
To lust and softness given, it strikes stark blind,
So the sly wandering factor...
But the sage, pious man, who still adores
And loves his Maker, and his love implores,
Whoever joys to search the secret cause
And series of his works, their love and laws,
Let him draw near, and joining will with strength,
Study this Art in all her depth and length;
Then grave experience shall his consort be
Skilled in large nature's inmost mystery.
The knots and doubts his busy course and cares
Will oft disturb, till time the truth declares,
And stable patience, through all trials passed,
Brings the glad end and long hoped for, at last.

(Heinrich Nolle, *The Chemist's Key;* translation from the
German, attributed to Henry Vaughan (1657).)

The alchemical operation works on three levels of being at once – on body, soul and spirit. The hermetic philosophy maintains that everything – animal, vegetable and mineral – contains these three elements, but in an unawakened form. The Great Work breaks down the existing relationship between them, activating each separately, and leading them from an ignorant and inert state to perfection. Alchemists initiate this operation both in the materials they work with in their laboratories and in their own individual being. They aim to free the soul and spirit of matter and to reunite them with the body in a new and exalted form; they also attempt to fulfil this task in their own lives.

Prayer, observation and work are the tools they use to activate their own spiritual, psychological and physical faculties.

Although all mainstream alchemy embodies this triple approach in principle, yet different schools and adepts have often chosen to emphasise one aspect in particular, and this engenders different qualities in the type of alchemy that results. Broadly speaking, alchemy emphasising the perfection of the body usually dwells more on metals and materials, the laboratory processes, and tangible results. This line of alchemy is the one most likely to give rise to chemical and scientific discoveries. Alchemy that gives the soul special consideration is likely to concern itself primarily with medicinal results and to seek for curative and healing agents – the art of the Elixir. It may use more vegetable than metallic matter in its work of preparation. Alchemy of the spirit put the greatest efforts into the illumination of individual minds, and may regard the physical and tangible results of alchemy as secondary. It lays emphasis on the role of contemplation within the alchemical work and tends to draw in religious and philosophical teaching. The effects of alchemy of body and soul will be considered in the next chapter; alchemy of the spirit will be the prime focus of this one.

Alchemy as spiritual development

To set the picture for a discussion of specific examples of spiritual alchemy, I shall give some indication of how the alchemical process works at a parallel level in the alchemist himself.

The Primal Material that the alchemical seekers take to work on at the spiritual level is their individual human self. Each person, say the teachings of alchemy, is made in the image of God and contains the seeds of soul and spirit within them. These seeds are, to some extent, imprisoned in the body; in order to release them that they may grow to perfection the seeker must summon up the will and intention to start the work and make the initial effort to dissolve this apparent unity. The body is not rejected as such, but it must be encouraged to loosen its hold upon the inner being so that the process of transformation can begin. This can be set in motion by embracing the alchemical discipline itself; the student decides to commit to a task that will demand the utmost in patience and concentration. The seeker's old way of life will be disrupted, since most of the available resources – money, time and mental effort – will be channelled into the alchemical work. There is no immediate gratification in terms of quick results, and

The Red Dragon, showing how the three forces innate in the Primal Material can be released (depicted as spheres tumbling out of the dragon's body), and then re-united in a perfect triangle, cradled in the union of sun and moon, at the close of the Great Work. (From George Ripley, circa 1600, MS Ashmole Rolls 53, The Bodleian Library, University of Oxford.)

no guarantee of success at all. Nor is there any turning back; the process both in the laboratory and in the human soul is considered irreversible. Although, in hermetic understanding, all first matter grows to gold in due course, and people evolve towards greater consciousness as part of a natural process, yet the change is usually too slow for individuals to perceive and experience: alchemy seeks to accelerate this change and bring about the possibility of completion within a personal life-span.

The labours of the alchemical work activate the faculties of such seekers, and the frustrations experienced in trying to find the right materials and correct sequence of operation will keep them alert and observant. The alchemists relate that when the initial dissolution has taken place, the Mercurial water can be extracted and reserved for future use. This 'water' corresponds to the elements of hope and faith the aspirants discover within themselves. All men and women have some intimation or experience of the divine in their lives, but sometimes this is locked away or rendered impotent by doubt. The first stage of dissolution allows a person to see this 'treasure' for what it really is. It should then be 'stored away' safely ready for later use, rather than subjected to the upheavals and even violence of the subsequent stages. Then, when there is resolution of the conflict (corresponding to the stage where the 'child' is born in the vessel), it can be added or released to nurture the growing creation with hope and love.

After the alchemical material has been prepared and put through the initial stages of dissolution and activation, it is heated in the sealed vessel. The sealed vessel corresponds to the secrecy with which the work is carried out, an important ingredient of spiritual discipline. Aspirants must be willing to keep their own counsel, confiding only in their teacher, if they have one – otherwise all is lost through evaporation or dissipation. (This is similar to the creative process in the arts, where it is advisable for the writer, musician or painter not to subject the work in progress to outside opinion until it is fully 'born', to prevent the inspiration and energy from disappearing completely.)

What is the heat that is applied to the vessel? In one sense, it is the student's aim, kept always to the fore, like a fire burning within. This corresponds to the 'burning love' of the mystics, without which they would lose heart and lack the courage to face the difficulties they encounter. In another way it can correspond to the friction caused by demanding tasks in the laboratory that stretch the alchemist to the limits of endurance. However, in alchemy it is stated that the heat must be carefully regulated, otherwise the vessel may crack and break: the energies the alchemist expends on laboratory work, research and religious prayer must all be tempered or else a harmful frenzy or mania can result.

In the apparatus, the liquid is circulated over and over again, being distilled and re-distilled to a degree that most scientists would consider pointless. The alchemists maintain that this is the only way to further the transformation of the material. If the action is performed with patience, attention and care, it will have results on the psychological level too. It is similar to certain religious and meditational practices, such as the orthodox Christian discipline of the 'prayer of the heart', which consists of repeating silently a short and simple prayer over and over again until it becomes a ceaseless and perpetual activity. Such repetitive practices are far from meaningless if carried out correctly, releasing potent and vital energies that will help to fuel the transformation.

This concept is made explicit in a Chinese book, *The Secret of the Golden Flower,* an alchemical-mystical text dating from around the eighth or ninth century AD. The work contains instructions for meditation based on the 'circulation of the light' within until it crystallizes into the Elixir:

> The Golden Flower is the light. What colour is the light?
> One uses the Golden Flower as a symbol. It is the true
> energy of the transcendent great One... When the light
> circulates, the energies of the whole body appear before
> its throne, as, when a holy king has established the
> capital and has laid down the fundamental rules of
> order, all the states approach with tribute... Therefore
> you have only to make the light circulate: that is the
> deepest and most wonderful secret. The light is easy to
> move, but difficult to fix. If it is made to circulate long
> enough, then it crystallizes itself; that is the natural spirit
> body... The Golden Flower is the Elixir of Life.

> (trans. Wilhelm 1965)

From its earliest recorded history, alchemy has contained all the ingredients necessary for a discipline that is to be practised within one's own being as well as in the laboratory retort. The process is described in terms of living beings – of dragons, fishes, birds, and of human archetypes, such as the king and queen, images which speak to us of our own elemental nature. The identification of the alchemist with his work is the chief distinction between alchemy and science, for while the scientist attempts to stand outside the experiment in order to obtain 'objective' results, the alchemist only values results that are obtained by personal effort and involvement.

Even the four elements of earth, water, fire and air must be brought into the correct balance in the personal realm; special attention is paid to the mastery of fire and water, for these two elements are contrary to one another in their action and are mutually destructive. The reconciliation of fire and water was a central aim in the process of perfection: 'The things that are in the realms above are also in the realms beneath; what heaven shows is often found on earth. Fire and flowing water are contrary to one another; Happy thou, if thou canst unite them: let it suffice thee to know this!' (frontispiece to *Musaeum Hermeticum* of 1625). This process was often symbolized by the Seal of Solomon, the double triangle interlaced with one apex pointing upwards and one down, representing the uniting of the heavenly and earthly principles.

The 'spiritual alchemists' frequently made much use of the doctrine of the three principles – mercury, salt and sulphur. In most alchemical texts it becomes obvious that mercury, as the soul, is the chief agent in alchemy, mediating between body and spirit and performing the transformations at each stage. Salt, the body, must perish and be resurrected, and sulphur, the spirit, must soar like the eagle and attain to knowledge.

> When he [Sulphur] is set free, he binds his gaolers, and gives their three kingdoms to his deliverer. He also gives to him a magic mirror, in which the three parts of the wisdom of the whole world may be seen and known at a glance: and this mirror clearly exhibits the creation of the world, the influences of the celestial virtues of earthly things, and the way in which Nature composed substances by the regulation of heat.
>
> (Michael Sendivogius, *The New Chemical Light,* in Waite 1893)

The texts show over and over again that knowledge and wisdom were devoutly sought by the alchemists: Sendivogius calls the alchemists 'the children of knowledge.' Sometimes the Great Work is illustrated in pictorial form as a mountain up which the seeker must climb, encountering dangers and trials at every turn of the path. The alchemist was often exhorted to search for the Primal Matter on the summit of a mountain:

> On the other side of the fourth leaf, he painted a fair flower on the top of a very high mountain, which was sore shaken with the north wind: it had the foot blue, the flowers white and red, the leaves shining like fine gold, and round about it the dragons and griffons of the North made their nests and abode...
>
> (Flamel 1624)

The words from Figure Forty of *The Book of Lambspring* show poignantly how the alchemist must aspire to the heights and then return to the earth to carry out for the Great Work:

> Here is an old father of Israel,
> Who has an only Son,

'Fermentation of the Sun and Moon.' Symbols are often combined in alchemical pictures in an intriguing and sometimes bizarre way. Here, the naked couple, dragons and toad represent specific elements of the alchemical process, which has reached the stage of fermentation. (MS of Elias Ashmole, Theatrum Chemicum Britannicum, seventeenth century., opp. p350, The Bodleian Library, University of Oxford.)

A Son whom he loves with all his heart.
With sorrow he prescribes sorrow to him.
He commits him to a guide,
Who is to conduct him withersoever he will.
The Guide addresses the Son in these words:
Come hither! I will conduct thee everywhere,
To the summit of the loftiest mountain,
That thou mayest understand all wisdom,
That thou mayest behold the greatness of the earth, and
    of the sea
And thence derived true pleasure.
I will bear thee through the air
To the gates of the highest heaven.
The Son hearkened to the words of the Guide,
And ascended upward with him;
There he saw the heavenly throne,
When he had beheld these things,
He remembered his Father with sighing,
Pitied the great sorrow of his Father,
And said: I will return to his breast.

The main body of alchemical literature thus contains symbolism which is potent enough to relate to human spiritual transformation, and is frequently explicit in its exhortations to the seeker to search for perfection and wisdom in his own being as well as in his laboratory experiments.

Alchemy and Christianity

In Europe, the tradition of spiritual alchemy became strongly identified with Christianity, and the alchemical operation was explained as the mystical path through which the individual could become one with Christ, who is himself the perfect Stone. The earliest source that draws the parallel between alchemy and Christianity is identified by C.G. Jung as the *Margarita Pretiosa*, written by Petrus Bonus of Ferrar in the fourteenth century. By the sixteenth and seventeenth centuries this approach had become well established, and authors exercised their metaphysical ingenuity in drawing correspondences between Christian and alchemical teaching.

In *The Sophic Hydrolith* the life of Jesus is equated with the transformation of the Stone in the alchemical process. The fire that

Father, Son and Guide here represent body, soul and spirit in perfect harmony, which the alchemist aims to achieve. (Figure 11 from The Book of Lambspring, *in Waite 1893.)*

heats the material is like the 'furnace of affliction' that Jesus had to pass through when he was rejected and insulted by men. The period of 'chemical digestion', the forty-day gestation period of the seed in the vessel, is like the forty-day-and-night fast that Christ spent in the wilderness. And the life of Christ has given us the elements we need for personal redemption, for his baptism and crucifixion are the water and spirit that will regenerate us when we have ourselves passed through the furnace and come to the 'true black Raven's head', the mortification when beauty and reputation are lost and intense suffering is experienced. This particular text shows that alchemy can be a truly spiritual and Christian discipline, while retaining a concern with practical alchemy.

111

Other writers, however, began to pay less attention to the laboratory aspects of the work and taught alchemy purely as a devotional and mystical discipline. The most famous of these is **Jacob Boehme** (1575–1624), whose writings are highly complex and enigmatic, containing descriptions of man's relationships to God and Christ couched in alchemical terms. Boehme's knowledge of alchemy was profound, but he began life as an untutored shoemaker having little concern for religious matters. The story of his conversion is related as follows:

> One day while tending his master's shoe shop, a mysterious stranger entered who, while he seemed to possess but little of this world's goods, appeared to be most wise and noble in spiritual attainment. The stranger asked the price of a pair of shoes, but young Boehme did not dare to name a figure, for fear that he would displease his master. The stranger insisted and Boehme finally placed a valuation which he felt was all that his master possibly could hope to secure for the shoes. The stranger immediately bought them and departed. A short distance down the street the mysterious stranger stopped and cried out in a loud voice, 'Jakob, Jakob, come forth'. In amazement and fright, Boehme ran out of the house. The strange man fixed his eyes upon the youth – great eyes which sparkled and seemed filled with divine light. He took the boy's right hand and addressed him as follows: 'Jakob, thou art little, but shalt be great, and become another man, such a one as at whom the world shall wonder.'
>
> (From the narrative of Manly Palmer Hall in McLean 1981c)

Boehme saw that the conflict induced between the warring elements in the alchemical vessel was an emblem of the activity of nature itself. Without conflict there could be no movement, no difference between created beings, and no motivation to bring about change and improvement.

This essential combat is to be cured finally by 'the light of nature' and by 'the desire of the spirit'. Boehme's summary of the alchemical spiritual work is as follows:

Some alchemical writings and illustrations have a strongly Christian flavour, as this one, with the implication of God in heaven at the top, and hell at the bottom. (From MS of Elias Ashmole, Theatrum Chemicum Britannicum, seventeenth century, opp. p350, The Bodleian Library, University of Oxford.)

[Man] lies now shut up after his fall in a gross,
deformed, bestial dead image; he is not like an angel,
much less like unto paradise; he is as the gross ore in
Saturn, wherein the gold is couched and shut up; his
paradisical image is in him as if it were not, and it is
also not manifest, the outward body is a stinking
carcass, while it yet lives in the poison; he is a bad
thorny bush, from whence notwithstanding fair rose-
buds may bloom forth, and grow out of the thorns, and
manifest that which lies hidden, and shut up in the
wrathful poisonful Mercury, till the artist who has made
him takes him in hand, and brings the living Mercury
into his gold or paradisical image disappeared and shut
up in death; so that the inclosed image, which was
created out of the divine meekness and love-essentiality,
may again bud and spring forth in the divine Mercury,
viz in the word of the Deity, which entered in the
humanity shut up...

And then the divine Mercury changes the wrathful
Mercury into its property, and Christ is born, who
bruises the head of the serpent... and a new man arises
in holiness and righteousness, which lives before God,
[and his divine image] appears and puts forth its lustre
as the hidden gold out of the earthly property.

(Boehme 1635 (1969: 13, 89))

Boehme's injection of alchemy into Christianity inspired many of the
mystics and thinkers who succeeded him.

Two other writers of the seventeenth century famous for their interest
in alchemy are **Henry and Thomas Vaughan**. The Vaughans were
twins, born in Breconshire in 1621, and both studied at Oxford.
Thomas, the lesser known of the two, had a colourful career as a
doctor, as a priest finally expelled from his living, and as an alchemist.
Henry, a fine mystical poet, read law and held the sedate post of
secretary to judge Lloyd. Thomas, interested in spiritual matters and a
keeper of a vivid dream diary, experimented and worked at alchemy
under the patronage of another famous 'chymist' of the day, Sir Robert
Murrey, Secretary of State for Scotland. He wrote frequently under the
pseudonym of 'Eugenius Philalethes'; his style is stirring, though he
lacks the polish of his more poetical brother. He exhorts us to follow
the path of Christianity as revealed through the alchemical teachings:

Truth calls to man: 'Be ye transmuted... be ye
transmuted from dead stones into living philosophical
stones. I am the true Medicine, rectifying and
transmuting that which is no more into that which it
was before corruption, and into something better by far,
and that which is not into that which it ought to be. Lo,
I am at the door of your conscience, knocking night and
day, and ye will not open unto me, yet I stand mildly
waiting... Come again and again, often come, ye who
seek wisdom... O sonorous voice, O voice sweet and
gracious to the ears of the sage, O fount of inexhaustible
riches to those thirsting after truth and justice! O solace
to the need of those who are desolate! Why seek ye
further, anxious mortals?'

(Vaughan 1888 (1974: 64))

Henry Vaughan, the poet, certainly understood the hermetic practice,
but it is not known to what extent he carried out alchemical
experiments. In his poetry he drew upon the mystical aspects of
alchemy: poems such as 'The Night', 'Cock-crowing', or 'A Vision of
Time and Eternity' provide convincing evidence that Vaughan was
using alchemy not simply as a literary device, but that he had a deep
understanding of its inner meaning and used this to fire his creative
work.

Father of lights! what sunny seed,
What glance of day hast thou confined
Into this bird? To all the breed
This busy ray thou has assigned;
    Their magnetism works all night,
    And dreams of Paradise and light.

Their eyes watch for the morning hue,
Their little grain expelling night
So shines and sings, as if it knew
The path unto the house of light,
    It seems their candle, howe'r done,
    Was tinned and lighted at the sun.

If such a tincture, such a touch,
So firm a longing can impower
Shall thy own image think it much
To watch for site appearing hour?

> If a mere blast so fill the sail,
> Shall not the breath of God prevail?

('Cock-crowing' in Vaughan 1976)

Alchemy and philosophy

From the late fifteenth century onwards, a general movement arose in European circles of learning and nobility that attempted to draw together all the strands of artistic, scientific and occult disciplines, and to weave them into one universal system of knowledge.

One major stimulus to the formation of a universal philosophy was the rediscovery of the hermetic texts in 1460. Cosimo de' Medici of Italy (see page 93) was at that time employing agents to scour the world for lost classics from the ancient Greek and Egyptian worlds. A monk presented him with a manuscript that proved to be a collection of many of the 'lost' texts ascribed to **Hermes Trismegistus,** a body of work now known as the *Corpus Hermeticum.* Hermes, closely associated with the Egyptian god Thoth, was said to have been a great Egyptian priest who had lived centuries before Christ. The writings under his name were widely revered, for here, it was thought, were the genuine and original teachings of Egypt, which apparently affirmed the truth of Christianity by referring to the existence of the divine Son.

Unfortunately, it was later discovered by Isaac Casaubon in 1614 that the texts did not predate Christ. We now know them to be the products of the first two or three centuries AD, composed by Greeks and containing strong Gnostic, Jewish and Neoplatonic influences. They may well contain elements of far earlier teachings, but they do not enshrine the wisdom of ancient Egypt. Nevertheless, even after 1614, they continued to exert a considerable fascination for alchemists and occult philosophers, the subtleties of observation and grandeur of cosmology being valued on their own account. They affirmed the principle of alchemy that Nature was the divine force of change operating within the Universe:

> The Kosmos also... has sense and thought; but its sense
> and thought are of a kind peculiar to itself, not like the
> sense and thought of man, nor varying like his, but
> mightier and less diversified. The sense and thought of
> the Kosmos are occupied solely in making all things,
> and dissolving them again into itself. The Kosmos is an
> instrument of God's will.

(*Corpus Hermeticum, Libellus II,* trans. Scott)

Man, the hermetic texts say, was created a being like God himself, made of Life and Light. He came to know the 'administrators', the planets that rule over destiny, and 'received a share of their nature'. But through will, he penetrated further into the created levels of the world, further into the realms of matter, until he was revealed to Nature. Nature fell in love with man, and enticed him to live on her Earth.

The task of Man is to have the courage and will to develop his powers and attain to knowledge:

> If then you do not make yourself equal to God, you
> cannot apprehend God; for like is known by like. Leap
> clear of all that is corporeal, and make yourself grow to
> a like expanse with that greatness which is beyond all
> measure; rise above all time and become eternal; then
> you will apprehend God. Think that for you too nothing
> is impossible; deem that you too are immortal, and that
> you are able to grasp all things in your thought, to know
> every craft and science; find your home in the haunts of
> every living creature; make yourself higher than all
> heights and lower than all depths, bring together in
> yourself all opposites of quality, heat and cold, dryness
> and fluidity; think that you are everywhere at once, on
> land, at sea, in heaven; think that you are not yet
> begotten, that you are in the womb, that you are young,
> that you are old, that you have died, that you are in the
> world beyond the grave; grasp in your thought all this at
> once, all times and places, all substances and qualities
> and magnitudes together; then you can apprehend God.
> But if you shut up your soul in your body, and abase
> yourself, and say 'I know nothing, I can do nothing; I
> am afraid of earth and sea, I cannot mount to heaven; I
> know not what I was, nor what I shall be', then what
> have you to do with God?
>
> (*Corpus Hermeticum, Libellus XI*, trans. Scott)

On this basis, there was nothing to be ashamed of in alchemy, for what was it but a search for God through his manifestations in Nature, carried out with the power of thought and skill of craft that God had bestowed on man so that he might understand better the secrets of the creation? In another respect, it did away with the old emphasis on choosing alchemy itself as a pathway, as a mistress the alchemist served with unceasing devotion. Men of learning chose more and more to combine occult arts and rational sciences in their quest for an ever wider worldview. They were not content to be bound by the obscure world of the laboratory and the daily attention to lengthy alchemical operations.

The opening up of alchemy, and its incorporation into new philosophies and schools of learning, meant that it provided a powerful leavening for the seekers of the period but became less and less distinguishable as a practice in its own right. For instance, it was a vital ingredient of Rosicrucianism, an esoteric movement that first came to prominence in 1614–15, when two texts – the *Fama Fraternitatis* and the *Confessio Fraternitatis* – appeared that told a strange tale of a secret society and a brotherhood that was ready to meet the dawning of a new age: 'Now there remains yet that which in short time... shall be spoke and uttered forth, when the World shall awake out of her heavy and drowsy sleep, and with an open heart, bare-head, and bare-foot, shall merrily and joyfully meet the new arising Sun.' The tale told in the *Fama* is that of one Brother Rosenkreuz who, a century or two before, had travelled widely in search of wisdom and learning and had founded an Order whose members were to devote themselves to this end.

The anonymous writer declared that the Order was still in existence, fortified by the recent discovery of the tomb of Rosenkreuz, which is described in precise and complex detail, indicating that it was laid out more as an occult temple than a grave. He implied that the Brethren were now seeking those of like mind to join them in preparation for the advent of wisdom into the world. The wisdom as formulated by the Order was to be of universal relevance, a synthesis of the best and most profound philosophy known to man. It would be 'a compendium of the Universe', the 'perfection [of] all Arts', 'so that finally man might thereby understand his own nobleness and worth, and why he is called Microcosmus, and how far his knowledge extendeth into Nature'.

The response was overwhelming. Many people wrote and published letters begging to be taken into the Order, while others condemned the heresy and presumption of the Brethren. No one openly admitted to being a member of the Order, but yet there soon grew up a body of literature and art that we can now classify as 'Rosicrucian'. It developed its own themes and identity, tying together kabbalism, Christianity, alchemy and astrology, as well as music, mathematics, geometry and architecture. As time went on, the reality of Rosicrucian

An alchemist and his assistants working in a laboratory. This traditional way of working on the alchemical process began to fall out of favour in the seventeenth century. (From a German alchemical poem, seventeenth century MS. Add. A. 287, p12, The Bodleian Library, University of Oxford.)

brotherhoods was more readily admitted (one of the most intriguing by name being an American branch entitled The Woman in the Wilderness, devoted chiefly to the practice of spiritual alchemy), but by the mid-eighteenth century the early freshness and vitality had gone out of the concepts and emblems.

The works of writers such as Michael Maier, Heinrich Khunrath and Robert Fludd typify Rosicrucian literature and show how alchemy played a large part in it. According to one authority, **Heinrich Khunrath,** although he died in 1605, before the official 'launch' of Rosicrucianism, 'bears within the compass of his books all the elements that we recognise later in the Rosicrucian publications.' (McLean 1981a) He was in contact with, among others, John Dee and Emperor Rudolf of Prague, both of whom are thought to form links in the Rosicrucian chain. His *Amphitheatre of Eternal Wisdom*, with its very fine engravings, is a good example of how Rosicrucian illustrations differed from those of traditional alchemy. The latter usually set out to illustrate each stage of the alchemical process in turn. The Rosicrucians tend to give a complete picture of the quest in each illustration, including as many aspects as possible. For instance, in the engravings 'The Journey to the Heights' and 'The Castle of the Mysteries', the whole search is shown from start to finish, with aspirants setting out, working, travelling by boat, meeting with others, contemplating, praying, and so on. The landscapes are complex, and symmetry, proportion and perspective are used to make symbolic points. Khunrath did not neglect alchemy proper. A laboratory is shown in detail in 'The First Stage of the Great Work', but the room is also equipped with an oratory (in which the aspirant is shown praying) as well as musical and mathematical equipment. Alchemy was thus no longer seen as an exclusive art; it was brought into line with other disciplines in order to create a harmonious philosophy.

The Rosicrucian manifestos mention alchemy by name, and they curse the blindness of those who seek gold as a goal in its own right. It is the province of 'many runagates and roguish people [who] use great villainies and cozen and abuse the credit which is given them.' Those who want merely to transmute metals are not true philosophers. But, their doctrines affirm, the pursuit of wisdom through alchemy is a sacred calling:

> Whatsoever has been said in the *Fama* ['The Fame'; see source below] concerning the deceivers against the transmutation of metals, and the highest medicine in the world, the same is thus to be understood, that this is so great gift of God we do in no manner set at naught, or despise it. But because she bringeth not with her always the knowledge of Nature, but this bringeth forth not only medicine, but also maketh manifest and open unto us innumerable secrets and wonders. Therefore it is requisite, that we be earnest to attain to the understanding and knowledge of Philosophy. And moreover, excellent wits ought not to be drawn to the tincture of metals, before they be exercised well in the knowledge of Nature.
>
> (Eugenius Philalethes (pseud.) *The Fame and Confession of the Fraternity of R.C. commonly of the Rosie Cross,* 1652, trans. Henry Vaughan, in Allen 1968: 187)

We have little evidence of how the Rosicrucians applied their philosophy and learning in terms of individual development. The only

Golden Lane in Prague, a street where alchemists are thought to have lived and worked.

clues come from writers who seem to bear the Rosicrucian identity, even if they do not admit to being one of the brotherhood. Such a one is **Robert Fludd** (1574–1637). He was the son of Sir Thomas Fludd, a military administrator, and was educated at Oxford. In 1598 he spent six years travelling as a tutor on the Continent, during which time he probably developed his medical and occult interests, partly through contact with Paracelsians (see Chapter Seven). He returned to England and took his degree in medicine, setting up practice in London, and was renowned for his successful personal effect upon his patients. But he came into conflict with the medical authorities because of his unorthodox views and his bluntness in expressing them. Fludd was celibate and devoted himself entirely to his medical practice and to his exploration, of philosophy through his knowledge of music, alchemy and science. His greatest work is the *History of the Macrocosm and the Microcosm*, in which he attempts to describe the divine and the human worlds and the way in which they interact.

Fludd did not openly admit to membership of the Rosicrucian Order, but he wrote an essay in their defence that expounded their virtues and the necessity of accomplishing the 'mystical building' of the rose and the cross for oneself:

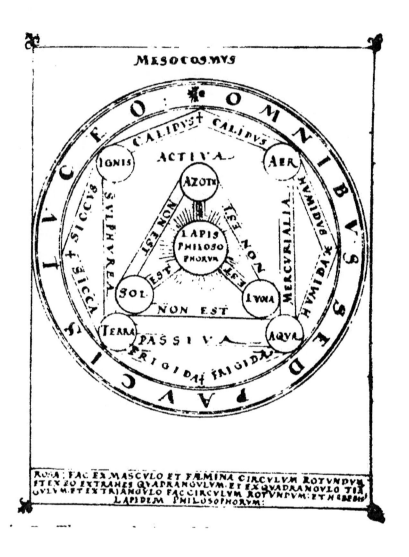

The completion of the Great Work is shown in geometric form; all
the elements are brought into harmony and the Philosopher's Stone
created. (From Sylva Philosophorum, a seventeenth-century work by
Cornelius Petraeus.)

The Alchemist transmutes the apparent forms into occult ones by finding the general form through destruction of the specific one. This is the work of the true and divine Alchemy, through the mediation of which the earthly has been opened to the entry of the joys of Paradise so that men may pluck that red rose with the lilies of the field and taste of the Tree of Life.

A spiritual, and Christian, form of alchemy, seems to have been a central theme for Fludd, and it may be that he distinguished this from 'laboratory' alchemy, which, in his diagrams, he lists equally with other arts and sciences, describing it only as 'art correcting Nature in the mineral realm.'

Alchemy thus expanded from a closely-knit discipline, into a tool for scientific and biological understanding, as well as into a spiritual teaching that was no longer dependent upon work carried out in a laboratory, and from the seventeenth century the history of 'pure' alchemy becomes harder to follow as it merges with other philosophies and traditions.

Chapter Seven

Applied alchemy

Alchemy has borne fruit in the realms of medicine, science and literature. Many of those who have been inspired by its philosophy and imagery were themselves practising alchemists, but often their alchemical skills have been overshadowed by their successes in the more conventional areas of the sciences and arts. There is a tendency to reject the tree which bore the fruit; the view is frequently taken by contemporary writers that the sole function of alchemy was to provide a starting point for the more 'objective' sciences. The more esoteric aspects of alchemy are often regarded as the necessary, but rather regrettable, means by which alchemy grew until it could be turned into a proper science. However since alchemy has been a source of inspiration for physicists, doctors, mystics, writers and psychologists, its power as a way of knowledge in its own right must surely be recognised. Alchemy rests on principles that have a deep relevance to man's work and progress in the world. The principles may be clothed in forms which are archaic or even erroneous in their assumptions, but these do not invalidate the principles themselves. Alchemy is like a central spindle, from which threads are unwound and taken into other contexts; they may eventually sever their original connection; but the spindle remains, and can be used again after years of neglect.

Paracelsus and alchemical medicine

Theophrastus Bombastus von Hohenheim (1493–1541), better known as **Paracelsus**, was born near Zurich and grew up in Villach (now in Austria). The whole course of his life was marked by an avid curiosity to learn at first hand, and to investigate and experiment without being tied to traditional doctrines. His first known phase of study began when he joined Sigismund Fugger, proprietor of mines and metal workshops in the Tyrol; here he learnt techniques of mining and the ways of using minerals and metals. Fugger himself was an alchemist, so alchemy was probably a very early topic of study for Paracelsus.

Training in occult matters may have come about as a result of contact with **Johannes Trithemius** (1462–1516), abbot of the monastery at Sponheim, an unusually learned and open-minded man who had been instructed in the secret sciences in his youth. He built up a magnificent library at the abbey; his own learning embraced the Kabbalah and Neoplatonic doctrines. As might be expected, he was at times accused of practising black magic, but he defended his position with the words: 'I am a lover of Divine Wisdom – in man and in Nature. This is the Magic I follow.' His pupils are thought to have included Cornelius Agrippa, the famous occultist and his writings such as the Steganographia, a treatise on angelic beings and astrology, were eagerly sought after by men such as John Dee.

We can infer from influences such as those of Fugger and Trithemius that Paracelsus was determined to expand his sphere of knowledge and bring the very highest and best into the medicine he practised. He also had a great respect for the native wisdom of peasants and gypsies, whom he saw as true observers of Nature. He had no respect for authority or academia, was badly dressed, frequently drunk, and always ready to quarrel. He travelled widely throughout Europe, possibly in the East as well, and his claim to have taken the last boat out from Rhodes before the Turkish invasion might link him with the Knights of St John (see page 67). His professional status reached its peak when he was offered the post of City Physician and Professor of Medicine at Basel University after he had cured Johann Froben, a well-to-do printer who had been suffering from a serious and perplexing illness.

But Paracelsus soon made himself unpopular by refusing to worship at the shrine of Galen, Avicenna and Aristotle, whose writings were accorded the authority of scripture by the medical practitioners of the day. He even burnt some of the sacred volumes in public and insulted the unquestioning physicians of his time in almost everything he wrote, calling them 'sausage-stuffers', 'clownish concocters', 'importers' and 'ignorant sprouts'! After an unhappy lawsuit, Paracelsus left Basel in a hurry and spent most of his remaining years travelling in Germany and Austria. After his death in 1541 his followers grew in number until by about 1570 a definite Paracelsian school existed, and his influence has since spread; he is now

Paracelsus, standing at the borders of alchemy and medicine, a rebel in his day, and a significant influence in the development of contemporary homeopathy and complementary medicine.

considered as a key figure in the birth not only of modern orthodox medicine but also of homeopathic medicine.

His writings are numerous and complex, and it is not clear which are original works and which were composed by his pupils. Today there is a tendency to label his interests separately as alchemy, astrology, pharmacy or magic, but Paracelsus considered that they all should interact if medicine was to be effective.

A key feature of Paracelsian alchemical medicine was the importance of celestial energies and influences. Planets and metals were closely associated; gold, for instance, was said to be influenced by the sun as it grew to perfection in the earth and was itself an emblem of solar power. Each metal was related to a specific planet and was said to contain within itself an 'arcanum', a celestial power derived directly from its ruling planet. This arcanum could be released and perfected through the alchemical process and then used as an effective medicine. Modern chemists view this as the first real attempt to select out the active ingredient in a substance through chemical processes.

Carrying out such alchemical work, Paracelsus maintained, was like recreating the universe in miniature. The right conditions in the vessel must be engendered so that the precise arcanum will manifest itself, just as the corresponding planet came to birth in the original creation

Frontispiece to one of Paracelsus's many treatises.

PARACELSUS

Of the

Supreme MYSTERIES

OF

NATURE.

Of {The Spirits of the Planets.
Occult Philofophy.

The Magical, Sympathetical, and Antipathetical CURE of Wounds and Difeafes.

The Myfteries of the twelve SIGNS of the ZODI-ACK.

Englifhed by R. Turner,
Φιλομαϑής.

London, Printed by *J. C.* for *N. Brook* and *J. Harifon*; and are to be fold at their fhops at the Angel in Cornhil, and the holy Lamb neer the Eaft-end of *Pauls.* 1656.

of the world. He said that the alchemical furnace should be made like the firmament itself, 'fit and apt for the motion of Matter.' Within this, the glass vessel is placed like an inner firmament, and inside this the desired creation may take place. The work of alchemy is not primarily to make gold and silver:

> Its special work is this – To make arcana, and direct these to disease... The physician... must judge the nature of Medicine according to the stars... Since Medicine is worthless save in so far as it is from heaven, it is necessary that it shall be derived from heaven... Know, therefore, that it is arcana alone which are strength and virtues. They are, moreover, volatile

substances, without bodies; they are a chaos, clear, pellucid, and in the power of a star.

(Paracelsus, *Alchemy: The third column of medicine* in Waite 1894)

Ordinary herbal brews, said Paracelsus, were unlikely to be of great value since medicine should be of a subtle and potent composition, the original substance having undergone genuine transformation. Man himself has a level of being that corresponds to the celestial; therefore, if he is ill harmony should be restored at this level rather than at the gross physical level only:

> The third fundamental part, or pillar of true medicine, is Alchemy. Unless the physician be perfectly acquainted with, and experienced in this art, everything that he devotes to the rest of his art will be vain and useless. Nature is so keen and subtle in her operations that she cannot be dealt with except by a sublime and accurate mode of treatment. She brings nothing to the light that is at once perfect in itself, but leaves it to be perfected by man. This method of perfection is called Alchemy. For the Alchemist is a baker, in that he bakes bread; a wine merchant, seeing that he prepares wine; a weaver, because he produces cloths. So, whatever is poured forth from the bosom of Nature, he who adapts it to that purpose for which it is destined is an Alchemist.

(Paracelsus, *Alchemy: The third column of medicine* in Waite 1894: 148)

Paracelsus taught that the body itself is an alchemist. It transforms food and uses the beneficial substances, eliminating the rest. Here again Paracelsus was ahead of his time from the scientific point of view in seeing a relationship between chemistry and biochemistry. And from alchemy, he took the principle that a poison may contain much that is good within it. Poison, he said, is a relative term: 'Remember that God has formed all things perfect, in so far as regards their utility to themselves, but imperfect to others. Herein rests the foundation of the entity of poison.'

Arguing that what could be a poison in its gross form could also be a powerful medicine when prepared correctly, he went against the traditional Galenic view of curing through opposites. He maintained that the arcanum of a substance could be used to cure the evil effects which the substance itself produced. This is echoed in modern homeopathy, where minute doses of a substance are given to cure symptoms that correspond to those that the same substance would provoke if taken in a larger quantity: Belladonna, for instance, in a homeopathic dilution, may be used to treat delirium and fever – standard symptoms of belladonna poisoning – even though the patient has not in fact taken belladonna in its normal form. Homeopathy also follows the attempt of Paracelsus to work in the subtler realms of matter and mind, since the doses are so diluted that they pass beyond the level of normal measurable chemical dosage and may be said to correspond, broadly speaking, to the Paracelsian 'quintessence' or arcanum of the matter and to affect, accordingly, a deeper level of the patient's metabolism, a level at which psyche and body interact.

Science and alchemy

Alchemy always maintained a connection with the more practical arts of pharmacy and metallurgy. Frequently, processes initiated in the alchemical laboratory have emerged eventually into the everyday world as significant discoveries. A fine example, drawn to our attention by Sherwood Taylor, is that of the distillation of alcoholic spirits. From about AD 100 until the thirteenth century, distillation was exclusively an alchemical process; pharmacists of the time only used extraction, rather than the chemical technique of vaporizing and condensing. In the early Middle Ages alchemy went a step further and distilled wine into *aqua ardens* – brandy, a commonplace to us, but a marvel when it was first discovered. It was a manifestation of the alchemical aspiration to combine the two elements of fire and water, for it was both liquid and inflammable. Its medicinal powers were also found to be great, stimulating warmth and recovery from shock. Alcoholic spirits could also be used to preserve other organic materials and to extract essential oils from plants.

A list of achievements contributed by alchemy to science is given in *The Morning of the Magicians* by Louis Pauwels and Jacques Bergier. They include:

+ the production of potassium lye by Albert le Grand (1193–1280)

+ the discovery of sodium sulphate by Johann Glauber (1604–68)

+ the discovery of benzoic acid by Blaise Vigenere (1523–96)

Woolsthorpe Manor, Isaac Newton's family home in Lincolnshire, at the time a modest sheep farm.

+ the recognition of gases by Johann-Baptiste Van Helmont (1577–1644)

+ the production of tin monoxide by G. della Porta (1541–1615).

The most potent and fascinating fusion of alchemy and science, however, came in the seventeenth and early eighteenth centuries with the work of eminent scientists such as Robert Boyle and Sir Isaac Newton. Both practised alchemy, both were inspired by its creed and both claimed to have achieved alchemical results. For these, and other scientists of the period, alchemy and science were bound up together, with alchemy influencing, and being influenced by, mechanical theories of matter, and science itself resting on a basis of mysticism and metaphysics. To the seventeenth-century mind, the worlds of nature, man and the divinity were inseparably related, and to study one without acknowledging the others was considered to be a distortion of the truth. **Sir Isaac Newton** (1642–1727) was born into a Lincolnshire family. A scholarly uncle took an interest in his education, sending him first to school at Grantham and then to Cambridge, where he eventually became a Fellow of Trinity College. His public reputation was high: he was made Warden of the Mint in 1696 and knighted in 1705, by which time he was also President of the Royal Society.

Newton's study, recreated at his country home Woolsthorpe Manor, where he formulated several of his revolutionary theories about mathematics, light, and planetary motion, after he returned there in 1665 to escape the plague in Cambridge.

Newton is best known now for his formulation of the theory of gravity, his discovery of the spectrum in white light, and his laws of planetary motion. But he was also a mystic and an alchemist, versed in hermetic teachings, the Kabbalah and Neoplatonism. He was probably in contact with Henry More and Isaac Barrow, who were themselves Neoplatonists and in touch with alchemical circles in London. Newton was a secretive and reserved man, and only through his numerous unpublished papers and scattered contemporary references can we access his alchemical thought and practice. He had a well-stocked library of alchemical books, and maintained his own laboratory. When a biography of Newton was being prepared after his death, his former assistant, Dr Humphrey Newton, ventured this reminiscence:

> He very rarely went to bed till two or three of the clock,
> sometimes not until five or six, lying about four or five
> hours, especially at spring and fall of the leaf, at which
> times he used to employ about six weeks in his
> laboratory, the fire scarcely going out either night or
> day; he sitting up one night and I another, till he had
> finished his chemical experiments, in the performances
> of which he was the most accurate, strict, exact. What
> his aim might be I was not able to penetrate into, but
> his pains, his diligence at these set times made me think
> he aimed at something beyond the reach of human art
> and industry... Nothing extraordinary, as I can
> remember, happened in making his experiments; which,
> if there did, he was of so sedate and even temper, that I
> could not in the least discover it.

(Quoted in Dobbs 1975)

(The references here to work in the spring and autumn correspond to the traditional alchemical times for starting the Great Work at the equinoxes.) But Newton *did* claim to have achieved success in making the philosophical mercury:

> I know whereof I write, for I have in the fire manifold glasses with gold and this mercury. They grow in these glasses in the form of a tree, and by a continued circulation the trees are dissolved again with the work into a new mercury. I have such a vessel in the fire with gold thus dissolved, where the gold was visibly not dissolved through a corrosive into atoms, but extrinsically and intrinsically into a mercury as living and mobile as any mercury found in the world. For it makes the gold begin to swell, to be swollen and to putrefy, and also to spring forth into sprouts and branches, changing colours daily, the appearances of which fascinate me everyday.

(Quoted in Dobbs 1975)

In other words, Newton was acknowledging current atomic theory of matter but was also stating that matter can be broken down in another way and that transformations can take place that by-pass the atomic process of combination.

Several of Newton's contemporaries brought alchemy out into the open and endeavoured to formulate its laws in the context of the new spirit of scientific enquiry. **Samuel Hartlib,** (*circa* 1600–62) a Prussian, who was resident in England after 1625, was the focus of a circle of keen experimenters who compared results and discussed metaphysical and scientific theories, trying to find a synthesis and a balance between them. A laboratory was set up in Hartlib's back kitchen and, in more gracious fashion, the enthusiasts also met at Ragley, the stately home of Lord and Lady Conway, who were keenly interested in such matters.

Robert Boyle (1627–91), moved away from the old, secretive, esoteric way of working, caused great concern to Newton by his frank and open attitude. Boyle thought that he too had succeeded in making philosophic mercury, but Newton prayed that he would keep silence, for such a secret was:

> ... not to be communicated without immense damage to ye world if there should be any verity in ye

A tree produced in the alchemical vessel, perhaps similar to the one that Isaac Newton claimed to have produced. (From Hieronymous Reusner Pandora, *1582)*

Hermetick writers.' Boyle's attitude was very different:
'[If] the Elixir be a secret, that we owe wholly to our
Maker's revelation, not our own industry, me thinks we
should not so much grudge to impart what we did not
labour to acquire, since our Saviour's prescription in the
like case was this: Freely ye have received, freely give.

(Quoted in Dobbs 1975: 108)

Boyle was later to write *The Sceptical Chymist,* in which he attacked
the classical view that matter consisted of the four elements and
substituted the definition of an element as that which cannot be broken
down into any further substances. Whether he considered that
alchemy was still a workable principle on this basis is uncertain. In
Newton's case, however, research has shown that his knowledge of
alchemy and hermeticism was a direct trigger for his discoveries in the
realm of physics (see Dobbs 1975). Without the study of alchemy and
mysticism, Newton could not have made the discoveries that he did;
nor did he consider that such discoveries invalidated the occult basis
of science.

Throughout the seventeenth century, and on into the eighteenth
century, isolated individuals struggled on to maintain their alchemical
interests in an increasingly sceptical world. Thomas Daunt VII kept a
magician's and alchemist's study at Owlpen Manor House in
Gloucestershire, where he practiced his arts in semi-seclusion, and
frightened the local inhabitants, many of whom believed that the place
was haunted as a result. On his death in 1803, the local parson was
sent for to destroy his devilish books. As they were set alight, so it was
said, birds flew out of the burning pages. Perhaps Owlpen had a
tradition of alchemical and mystical working, since its grounds also
include the remains of a garden created on seven levels, to represent
the ascent of the seven stages of Paradise or the seven planets, both
familiar concepts in alchemy.

Chemistry took over from alchemy the accumulated knowledge of
laboratory equipment, of chemical processes such as distillation,
sublimation and coagulation, and all the formulas, materials and
techniques that dealt exclusively with the physical properties of matter
and identifiable chemical changes. Alchemy had been based upon
personal effort, religious devotion and revelation, whereas the new
chemistry took as its criteria experiments that could be repeated and
theories that could be considered as proven only when identical
results happened under identical conditions. Chemistry took the

A view showing Owlpen Manor in Gloucestershire, where the magician and alchemist Thomas Daunt VII practised, and the last vestiges of a garden dedicated to the planets, sun and moon.

principle of careful observation from alchemy, but denied that the observer could affect the experiment or be involved in it. From the mid-eighteenth century onwards, anyone who tried to mix alchemy and chemistry was courting disaster. The unfortunate James Price, commanded to prove the transmuting powers of a powder which he claimed changed mercury into gold, committed suicide by swallowing prussic acid rather than face the sceptical eyes of the Fellows of the Royal Society.

There is no doubt that alchemy could not be called an objective science, as science was defined in the eighteenth and nineteenth centuries. But with contemporary science now undergoing a radical shift of viewpoint, and with our fundamental notions of the realities of time, space and matter all being revised and gaining – once more – a metaphysical aspect, alchemical concepts may yet provide future science with insights into the nature of the universe.

Alchemy and literature

The drama of the alchemical process made fine material for literary adaptation. The essence of drama is conflict, and in alchemy conflict leads to transformation through a sequence of different states. The themes of elemental conflict, death of the body, the triumphal union of the king and queen, and the growth of a precious elixir could serve as a structure for expressions of love, tragedy and Christian revelation. On a lighter note, the delusions of the naive alchemist and the trickery of the fraudulent transmuter provided material for satirical comedy, the most famous example of which is *The Alchemist* by **Ben Jonson** (1572–1637). However much Jonson may have ridiculed alchemy, he knew his subject well and could play with its images and implications in an intricate and subtle fashion, as Charles Nicholl has shown in *The Chemical Theatre* (Nicholl 1980). Moreover, in *Eastward Hoe* Jonson and his co-authors used alchemical principles to provide a psychological structure for the drama; the characters of Frank Quicksilver, Master Golding and William Touchstone are defined by the alchemical associations with their names. Nicholl says:

> The naming of Quicksilver and Golding is not only a means of defining what they are... but of suggesting what will happen to them. It also provides a formula for interaction, for as well as having individual chemical properties, mercury and gold had a specific relationship. By introducing a symbolic framework of chemical process and reaction, the authors of Eastward Hoe [Jonson, Marston and Chapman] turn the essentially static humour-portrayal into an active participant in the play's unfolding.

> (Nicholl 1980)

There are strong indications that **William Shakespeare** (*circa* 1564–1616) also used alchemy to give form and texture to his dramatic themes in certain plays. There is no doubt that he was acquainted with occult traditions (see Yates 1979); he was well-versed in the Christian Kabbalah, astrology, magic, and it seems, alchemy. To what extent Shakespeare practised any of these subjects is debatable, but clearly he had enough insight to weave them skilfully into his writing.

A Midsummer Night's Dream, for instance, can be interpreted successfully as an alchemical drama, as the Theatre Set-Up company proved in their research and 1983 production. Their conclusion was that Shakespeare used a heady mixture of Celtic lore and alchemy to give the *Dream* its enchanting quality. Programme notes point to the theme of the four lovers, who to reach true harmony and a proper

*The golden serpent
represented on a plaque
in Prague, where alchemy
was practised intensively
in the sixteenth and
seventeenth centuries.
Many buildings there still
bear alchemical emblems
today.*

relationship must first be set in conflict with one another, just as the first material must be broken down if it is to be transformed:

The 'subject matter' or 'raw stuff' (often symbolized by a serpent, dragon or toad and called 'earth' or 'lead') was thought to consist of the elements fire, air, water and earth. These appear in the names of the four lovers; fire in 'Helen' (torch of reeds), air in 'Hermia' (female of Hermes – the Greek for Mercury, whose element was air), water in 'Lysander' (from the chemical loosening as in catalyst – hence the liquid vitriol and water), and earth in 'Demetrius' (son of Demeter, earth-goddess), who thus becomes a subject matter of alchemical process. Helen as fire (often symbolized as a dog – hence 'I am your spaniel') is also his soul (symbolized as a dove, which she is called) or anima from which he must be separated, while his 'grossness' is purged and his change tested until he can be re-animated, as an improved person, and awaken to a 'golden dawn of concluding harmony.'

There are three sets of weddings in the play: that of Theseus and Hippolyta, the royal pair, that of the two couples just discussed, and then the union of Titania and Oberon, who had become estranged. This too is resonant with alchemical allegory, and the three levels can be seen as body, soul and spirit, all of which must complete the perfect change if the alchemical process is to succeed. The union of Titania and Oberon may be interpreted as representing the body, since they are themselves nature spirits, that of the four lovers as signifying the soul (which in alchemy needs the most careful and complex handling), and that of the royal pair as the spirit. The spirit, or 'sulphur', requires less transformation than the other two, needing rather to be brought out from obscurity and affirmed just as Hippolyta, Queen of the Amazons, has been led out from her fierce and distant country by Theseus. Puck is the means by which all the trouble is stirred up, the cause of mischief and misunderstanding:

> The agent of alchemy was Mercury, who 'led' the subjects and practised upon them, beginning and finishing the work. This is Puck's function and psychologically he is the 'psychopomp' leading the souls, like Virgil in Dante's *Inferno*.

(Theatre Set-Up programme notes, 1983)

Mercury was depicted as totally volatile, changeable and elusive, taking the symbolic forms of different beasts, birds and figures in alchemical illustration. This corresponds precisely to Puck's gleeful speech when he upsets the rustics at their play rehearsal and scatters them into flight in the forest.

> I'll follow you, I'll lead you about a round,
> Through bog, through bush, through brake, through
>   brier:
> Sometimes a horse I'll be, sometime a hound,
> A hog, a headless bear, sometimes a fire;
> And neigh, and bark, and grunt, and roar, and burn,
> Like horse, hound, hog, bear, fire, at every turn.

So through the powers of Mercury, unleashed by the alchemist (in this case perhaps corresponding to Oberon, who is Puck's master), the four elements are set at war with one another, and then reunited in perfect balance. Titania is humbled and overcomes her pride to become Oberon's consort once more; the three levels of marriage take place and the work is perfected.

In Shakespeare's *King Lear*, Charles Nicholl similarly detects another alchemical theme, with Lear himself as the subject of transformation through his renunciation of power, paternal love and even his sight. His mortification is complete, his own death is the ultimate tragedy, yet through his trials and death evil has been purged from the kingdom. The concluding 'golden' harmony is not as obvious in King Lear as in *A Midsummer Night's Dream*, but alchemical purgation of the gross and exalting of the fine has indeed taken place. Nicholl points out that Lear's daughter, Cordelia, is like the alchemical

This emblem depicts the essential triplicity of alchemy, (represented by the fishes as soul and spirit, swimming in the sea of the body), which may have been consciously used by Shakespeare in A Midsummer Night's Dream. Figure 1 from The Book of Lambspring: *(in Waite 1893)*

material that is despised and mistaken for poison, and yet is the most precious balm of all. Dismissed from the scene early on, she is like the portion of Mercurial water that must be reserved in the alchemical work until it is needed for restoration and nurturing of the injured, mortified matter (Nicholls 1980). Her tears, flowing for her father, are like the alchemical dew that is impregnated with powerful natural force:

> All bless'd secrets,
> All you unpublish'd virtues of the earth,
> Spring with my tears!
>
> (*King Lear* IV, iv)

Later, her kisses are seen as a healing balm:

> O my dear father! Restoration, hang
> Thy medicine on my lips, and let this kiss
> Repair those violent harms that my two sisters
> Have in thy reverence made!

(*King Lear*, IV, vii)

A more overt use of alchemical imagery can be found in the poetry of the sixteenth and seventeenth centuries: **John Donne** (1573–1631) frequently utilised alchemical themes in his work. In 'A Nocturnall upon S. Lucie's Day' he compares his state to that of the material that has absorbed light and moisture and now lies blackening in the vessel, dying to be reborn as the elixir:

> Study me then, you who shall lovers bee
> At the next world, that is, at the next Spring:
> For I am every dead thing,
> In whom love wrought new Alchimie.
> For his art did expresse
> A quintessence even from nothingnesse,
> From dull privations, and leane emptinesse
> He ruin'd mee, and I am re-begot
> Of absence, darknesse, death; things which are not.

George Herbert (1593–1633) and **Andrew Marvell** (1621–78) also used hermetic allusions in their verse, Herbert often in a simple and devout form, Marvell in a more speculative and philosophical vein. Herbert, for instance, begins his poem 'Easter' with the following lines:

> Rise, heart; thy Lord is risen. Sing his praise
> Without delays,
> Who takes thee by the hand, that thou likewise
> With him may'st rise;
> That, as his death calcined thee to dust,
> His life may make thee gold, and much more, Just.

One of the finest examples of a religious poem using alchemical symbolism is by **Robert Southwell** (*circa* 1561–95), who in 'The Burning Babe' saw the alchemical furnace as giving birth to Christ:

> As I in hoarie Winters night stoode shivering in the
> snow,
> Surpris'd I was with sodaine heate, which made myhart
> to glow;

This alchemical emblem of a king sweating out a deadly fever has resonance with the stricken King Lear in Shakespeare's play, and his drops of sweat are another version of the tears which his daughter Cordelia sheds to heal him. Figure 14 from The Book of Lambspring: *(in Waite 1893)*

And lifting up a fearefull eye, to view what fire was
    neare,
A pretty Babe all burning bright did in the ayre appeare;
Who scorched with excessive heate, such floods of
    teares did shed,
As though his floods should quench his flames, which
    with his teares were bred:
Alas (quoth he) but newly borne, in fierie heates I frie,
    Yet none approach to warme their harts or feele my
    fire, but I;

My faultless breast the furnace is, the fuell wounding
    thornes:
Love is the fire, and sighs the smoake, the ashes, shames
    and scornes;
The fewell Justice layeth on, and Mercie blowes the
    coales,
The metall in this furnace wrought, are mens defiled
    soules:
For which, as now on fire I am to worke them to their
    good,
So will I melt into a bath, to wash them in my blood.
    With this he vanisht out of sight, and swiftly shrunk
    away,
And straight called unto minde, that it was Christmasse
    day.

Chapter Eight
The phoenix:
Alchemy in the twentieth century

The history of alchemy in the twentieth century is a fragmented one. Firstly, there has been a continuation of the practice of traditional alchemy; secondly an absorption of alchemy into esoteric teachings; thirdly, a reappraisal of alchemy in terms of psychology; and fourthly, an effort to relate alchemy to the frontiers of science. Let us look at each of these stories in turn.

Traditional alchemy

Although traditional alchemy fell into a decline during the eighteenth and nineteenth centuries, it did not die out altogether. In the Islamic culture, especially, it was still practised in the time-honoured fashion. E.J. Holmyard, an expert on Islamic alchemy, relates that he was acquainted with certain twentieth-century practitioners, one of whom was a learned theologian named Abdul-Muhyi (he came to England and carried out his experiments, unsuccessfully it seems, in a blacksmith's forge in Surrey). Muhyi had contacts with alchemical circles: 'One of his last acts', wrote Holmyard, 'was to write a letter of introduction to an alchemist friend at Fez, the outcome of which was to give the author the privilege of being taken to see a subterranean alchemical laboratory in the old part of the city.' More than this, one surmises, he was not allowed to divulge.

Since the general opinion in Europe from the eighteenth century onwards was that alchemy was the occupation of lunatics and impostors, those who have carried out alchemical studies in the twentieth century have tended to keep quiet about their activities. Two of the best accounts of modern alchemy are by Armand Barbault and

Archibald Cockren, both of whom seem to have come to alchemy from inner promptings, using historical texts for guidance, rather than by learning the discipline directly from a teacher.

Archibald Cockren's *Alchemy Rediscovered and Restored* (1940) contains a brief and over-generalised history of alchemy, but of far greater interest is a section in which he recounts his own alchemical experiments and eventual success. He worked with different metals over many years until he found the right one (unnamed) with which to begin the process of making the philosophical mercury:

> This metal, after being reduced to its salts and undergoing special preparation and distillation, delivered up the Mercury of the Philosophers, the Aqua Benedicta, the Aqua Celestis, the Water of Paradise. The first intimation I had of this triumph was a violent hissing, jets of vapour pouring from the retort and into the receiver like sharp bursts from a machine-gun, and then a violent explosion, whilst a very potent and subtle odour filled the laboratory and its surroundings. A friend has described this odour as resembling the dewy earth on a June morning, with the hint of growing flowers in the air, the breath of the wind over heather and hill, and the sweet smell of the rain on the parched earth.

> (Cockren 1940)

Cockren then had to find a way of storing this subtle and volatile gas; he managed to condense it into a 'clear golden-coloured water'. Later, he added this to salts of gold and through distillation of the mixture obtained oil of gold, or potable gold. To obtain the white and the red elixir, further stages were necessary, which involved treating the black metallic residue left after the extraction of the golden water and calcining it. Cockren calls this the 'salt', to which he added the 'mercury' and the 'sulphur', these being the white and the red water he had obtained from the golden mercurial water. He mixed the three principles in appropriate quantities, sealed them into a flask, and subjected them to a regulated heat. I quote here from his description of the change in the vessel, since it corresponds very closely with Newton's account (see page 132):

> On conjunction the mixture takes on the appearance of a leaden mud, which rises slowly like dough until it throws up a crystalline formation rather like a coral

plant in growth. The 'flowers' of this plant are composed of petals of crystal which are continually changing in colour.

From this point the process goes through the familiar stages of nigredo, conjunction, birth of the 'son', peacock's tail and finally the white then the red elixir.

Cockren was known to his contemporaries as a sincere and intelligent man; in addition he had a first-class professional scientific training, being a specialist in the field of physiotherapy and massage. His chief interest in alchemy was in its medical applications, and he follows Paracelsus in believing that all true medicine must be derived from purified substances, materials that have 'passed by fire to a second birth'.

Armand Barbault (1906–82), a Frenchman, also regarded the greatest good of alchemy as the production of effective medicine. He seems to have been of a very different character from Cockren, however – something of a cult figure, a showman magician-alchemist as opposed to the retiring and shy Cockren. His approach to alchemy is more original, and although he claimed to follow the signs and indications given in old texts and illustrations, he interpreted them very much in his own way. His account in *Gold of a Thousand Mornings* makes worthwhile reading, and brings out some interesting alchemical implications, especially concerning the role of astrology and the power of plants; but taken as a whole it is less convincing and definitely hovering more 'on the edge of the etheric' than Cockren's work.

Barbault worked almost exclusively with organic matter. His Primal Material, which he called the 'Philosopher's Peat', had to be gathered under correct locational and astrological conditions from about ten centimetres underneath the surface:

> What is this First Matter hidden several centimetres under the turf? Is it not – at least as far as the layman is concerned – plain ordinary earth? For the initiated person it is something quite different: it is living earth, seized from the ground by a very special process belonging to the sphere of High Magic, which allows the adept assigned to the task to gain possession of an entire collection of physical and metaphysical principles.

Barbault took much time and trouble gathering plants and dew for alchemical processing and for adding to the First Matter. Again, he was always careful that the time of day, the season and the planetary configurations were favourable so that the sap and the dew would be at maximum potency. Barbault had at one time been a fashionable professional astrologer, and he assessed each critical moment in the Great Work in detail, choosing a suitable horoscope for starting each stage of the process. Following the alchemical tradition he also believed that the practitioner's own chart was of vital importance. His horoscope, he boasted, proclaimed his special aptitude for a spiritualised science!

Barbault eventually perfected his elixir, and invited various professionals to test it, including the Weleda laboratories. The 'vegetable gold' apparently had extremely beneficial effects upon a number of patients suffering from different illnesses. He would have liked to have initiated full-scale production, but found that the cost of the operation needed was prohibitive. His conclusion was that his medicine was in a different category altogether from conventional medicine, although it had some connection with homoeopathic preparations:

> [I realised] that my liquor of gold was not a specific remedy but a universal additive, able to stimulate the effects of ordinary medicine to a remarkable degree by acting on the entire vital field. My medicine does not, therefore, seek to operate on the same wave-length as official medicine.

> (Barbault 1975)

Alchemical teachings were absorbed into a number of twentieth-century esoteric teachings. Some occultists, like Barbault, saw in alchemy a potential magical framework, its ceremonial approach and vivid mythological imagery lending itself to the development of psychic abilities and the harnessing of subtle energies. Magic can be briefly defined as the process of learning to understand, manipulate and interpret energies that exist in ourselves and in the natural world. Most students of magical traditions would agree that magic itself is 'natural', but involves working at a higher level of awareness and sensitivity than normal; it involves great personal responsibility and unless practised with proper motivation and discrimination, can become tainted with greed or delusion. In these broad terms, alchemy has a great affinity with magic in its emphasis upon releasing the active

Four astrological charts, redrawn from Norton's Ordinall of Alchemy; *the configuration of planets within the celestial zodiac has always been considered of great importance by alchemists. (From Elias Ashmole,* Theatrum Chemicum Brittanicum, *1652.)*

energy from material substances through the dedication and correct outlook of the practitioner.

The Hermetic Order of the Golden Dawn incorporated alchemy into its occult teachings. The Order was founded in 1887, and was intensively active in the first two decades of the twentieth century; its influence may be perceived in many esoteric orders today. The Order is said to have had Rosicrucian affiliations, but its origins are shrouded in myth and mystery like its purported antecedent. The Order was carefully structured, conducted on a basis of ordered learning programmes for its initiates, who moved up from one grade to another as they mastered various systems and skills. The Kabbalah was taught, as was divination – mainly astrology and tarot. Symbols were painted, magical weapons made, robes sewn and complex rituals learnt by heart.

Those who wished to proceed through the Order's grades were expected to be familiar with alchemical symbolism and perhaps to have some experience of practical alchemy. With its emphasis on divination, symbolism and experience of 'higher planes', the Golden Dawn concentrated more on the revelations that alchemy could bring rather than on its physical process. An instruction, probably written by S. L. MacGregor Mathers, a Chief of the Order, reads as follows:

> Before commencing any Alchemical process, and at the different stages of it, bring the Cucurbite, Retort, Crucible, or other vessel containing the Matter, place it in the centre of the table and range the Tablets round it thus: White Tablet with Head (North), Black and Grey Tablet with white pentacle (East), Tablet with Crystal (South), Coloured Tablet with Hexagram (West). (The Operator stands in the South.)

> Then endeavour according to the directions to see in the Crystal and go to the Alchemical plane corresponding under the Sephira of (Chokmah) where ask the Governor of Hylech to send down the Divine Light into the Matter, the LVX. Perform what other operations you wish and then remove the Tablets and continue the Alchemical processes as usual. In the intervals between the stages etc., act as here prescribed.

> Description of the Plane. A beautiful garden in which is a fountain issuing from a pillar and filling a large oblong

basin with a certain white water. This place is guarded
by an Angel with a Caducean Wand, who represents
Metatron on this plane. Ask him to bring you before the
Throne of the Governor of Hylech. Above the Pillar is a
Globe and the Bird of Hermes human-headed. Further
on is the throne of the Governor of Hylech who has
rainbow colours about him. There are also near him the
four Angels of the Elements, the Red King and White
Queen etc. and many other symbolic forms. Ask the
Governor of Hylech that the Divine LVX may be sent
into the Matter and give as your symbols (the Pyramid)
and (the Rose Cross).

(Gilbert 1983)

Probably the most important contribution that the Golden Dawn made
to the alchemical tradition was in drawing out the potential of its
symbolism, and in acknowledging its position as an integral part of the
Western occult tradition. Without the Golden Dawn, quite possibly
alchemy would have been quietly pensioned off. The Golden Dawn
has imbued many Western spiritual and occult disciplines today with
some of the symbolism and terminology of alchemy. For instance,
following the path of knowledge is often referred to as the 'Great
Work', or simply 'the Work'. Modern descriptions of the Kabbalistic
Tree of Life, too, draw on alchemical practice. The diagram of the Tree
contains at its middle level a relationship between three points –
Tiphareth (individuality), Geburah (judgement and strength) and
Chesed (love and mercy), and it is often said that this triad is like a
vessel in which the soul must be born after a man is purified by being
stripped of false values and judgements and becoming receptive to the
true quality of love.

G.I. Gurdjieff also presented the basic ideas of alchemy in his 'work',
and used them in an original and inventive form. Gurdjieff was active
first in Russia, then in France and America from the early years of the
present century until his death in 1949. His teachings are hard to
summarise but, like those of the Golden Dawn, have had a profound
effect upon contemporary esoteric thinking and practice. They might
best be described as 'a science of consciousness', the teaching of a
way through which people can 'wake up' to their possibilities through
proper self-observation and the world around and through effective
direction of personal energies and emotions.

Gurdjieff taught that man possessed several 'centres' of consciousness, ranging from one of powerful instinct to ones of higher intellect and emotion. The body is not to be seen as a separate entity, but is connected to all these centres in specific and often subtle ways – the body is dense matter, whereas spirit is also matter, although very rarefied. He demonstrated that the body is a kind of factory that will convert the food that comes in to nourish itself. However, he did not restrict this to the notion of physical food, but taught that we take in three kinds of food: physical nourishment, air and impressions. We need all of these to stay alive. This Gurdjieff described as our own alchemy, the process by which we sift out the different elements and convert them into a form in which we can digest, store or use them in our physical, mental and emotional lives:

> This is our inner alchemy, the transmutation of base metals into precious metals. But all this alchemy is inside us, not outside... In man's inner alchemy higher substances are distilled out of other, coarser material which otherwise would remain in a coarse state. (Ouspensky 1957 (1986: 220))

Psychology and alchemy

In the field of psychology, alchemy has found a natural home. With the growing urge to explore human instincts and mental processes, it became apparent that the alchemical process could be seen as a description of inner transformation. While C.G. Jung (1875–1961), the Swiss psychologist, is the most famous interpreter of alchemy in this light, he was preceded by Major-General E.A. Hitchcock (1798–1870), an American who scorned the idea that the transmutation of metals was the true aim of alchemy, holding instead that 'man was the subject of Alchemy; and that the object of the art was the perfection, or at least the improvement, of man!' (Luther 1975)

Jung, however, is the most significant figure in the revival of alchemy in the twentieth century. Many people owe their interest in alchemical symbolism to his work, and his contribution to unlocking the language of alchemical emblems in terms of the human psyche cannot be over-valued. However, it would be short-sighted to assume that alchemical evolution comes to a halt with Jung; questions of the interaction of mind and matter were largely left untouched by him, and he had no interest in the actual laboratory operations of the alchemists.

The Great Work of alchemy, here shown as a synthesis of astrology and Kabbalah as well, an approach taken by various esoteric teaching schools in recent centuries. (From L. Thurneisser zum Thurn, Quinta Essentia, *1574.*)

Jung established the vital link between psychology and alchemy, and saw the imagery of alchemy as a description of the journey of the human soul. He discovered a profound correspondence between alchemical emblems and imagery occurring spontaneously in dreams, especially those that mark times of crisis or transformation for the dreamer. In some of his patients' dreams he found an almost precise parallel with images used in old alchemical illustrations, even though the patients concerned had no knowledge of alchemy. His basic theory, which has deeply influenced many therapists, artists, writers and thinkers ever since, is that the psyche of each person merges, at its deepest point, with the psyche of mankind as a whole (the 'collective unconscious') and that the human psyche – energy in its essence – crystallises into various fundamental images, which are beyond pictorial image in themselves ('archetypes') but which may surface in the form of a recognisable image or symbol in the consciousness of individual man, chiefly through the medium of dreams and visions. Jung saw that the alchemical symbols (such as the rose, the eagle, the king and queen, the fighting dragons) were themselves representatives of these archetypes and that the alchemists had, by means of these symbols, described the development of the human psyche itself from its 'raw' state into one of perfection, or gold.

Jung named this whole process 'individuation', and in doing so broke away from the prevalent theory that signs of disturbance in the individual were necessarily warnings of abnormality; he maintained that, like the alchemical process, the process of individual growth was one of conflict, crisis and change. He discovered that he could interpret certain of his patients' dreams as parallels of alchemical stages, and assess their current psychic state accordingly.

Jung was always willing to explore aspects of his own psyche, and to be affected by dreams and images. His discovery of alchemy emerged as part of his own personal development:

> Before I discovered alchemy, I had a series of dreams
> which repeatedly dealt with the same theme. Beside my
> house stood another, that is to say, another wing or
> annex, which was strange to me. Each time I would
> wonder in my dream why I did not know this house,
> although it had apparently always been there. Finally
> came a dream in which I reached the other wing. I
> discovered there a wonderful library, dating largely from
> the sixteenth and seventeenth centuries. Large, fat folio

Images such as these fascinated Jung; he saw in them symbols which stood for integration of the psyche. (From Rosarium Philosophorum, 1550.)

volumes, bound in pigskin, stood along the walls. Among them were a number of books embellished with copper engravings of a strange character, and illustrations containing curious symbols such as I had never seen before. At the time I did not know to what they referred; only much later did I recognize them as alchemical symbols. In the dream I was conscious only of the fascination exerted by them and by the entire library.

(Jung 1963)

Through his contact with alchemy Jung transformed his own understanding of Christianity:

One night I awoke and saw, bathed in bright light at the foot of my bed, the figure of Christ on the Cross. It was not quite life-size, but extremely distinct and I saw that this body was made of greenish gold. The vision was marvellously beautiful, and yet I was profoundly shaken by it... [It] came to me as if to point out that I had overlooked something in my reflections: the analogy of

Christ with the *aurum non vulgi* and the *viriditas* of the
alchemists... The green gold is the living quality which
the alchemists saw not only in man but also in organic
nature. It is an expression of the life-spirit, the *anima
mundi* or *filius macrocosmi*, the *Anthropos* who
animates the whole cosmos. This spirit has poured
himself into everything, even into inorganic matter; he is
present in metal and stone. My vision was thus a union
of the Christ-image with his analogue in matter, the
filius macrocosmi.

(Jung 1963)

In Jung we have an example of a man whose life and work was totally
transformed by contact with the alchemical tradition. He could be
called an alchemist of the psyche, the guiding Mercurius spirit who
could lead men and women through the dangers and trials of the inner
process of transformation.

Science and alchemy, or 'parachemistry'

The place of alchemy in modern science is hardly a prominent one.
However both the revival of interest in alchemy as a practical occult
discipline and the advances of the scientific world view mean that it
retains a foothold there. Alchemy has its modern practitioners;
although the cutting edge of scientific discovery, with all its
sophisticated equipment, can hardly be exercised in one's back
parlour; nevertheless there is a place for those who wish to try and
integrate qualities of attention and inner vision with laboratory work.
Likewise, in the field of complementary medicine, experiments are
being conducted in the preparation of medicines with these principles
in mind, processes in which prevailing planetary influences and state
of mind of the operator are considered as having a potential influence
on the efficacy of the remedy.

Whether alchemy can achieve physical results unknown to
conventional science remains a moot point; certain twentyfirst-century
adepts believe that it has as much power to wield as nuclear physics.

In *The Morning of the Magicians*, Jacques Bergier relates his account of
a meeting in 1937 with a 'mysterious personage', an impressive and
practising alchemist who warned him of the dangers of nuclear
science, which was then in a critically expansive phase. He told
Bergier that such experiments were fraught with dangers through

The Green Lion, symbol of the living force that must be sought in the Primal Material, perhaps relating to Jung's vision of the green-gold Christ figure. (Emblem 37, Michael Maier, Atlanta Fugiens, 1617.)

explosive release of atomic energy and poisoning through radiation. His most startling pronouncement was that the alchemists themselves were in possession of this secret and had used the nuclear principle in their work for centuries – aeons, perhaps – but had done so from 'moral and religious' motivations, which had enabled them to handle the power in a responsible way. Bergier, who had been longing to meet a genuine alchemist, asked the stranger to instruct him as to the true nature of the art:

> You ask me to summarize for you in four minutes four thousand years of philosophy and the efforts of a life-time. Furthermore, you ask me to translate into ordinary language concepts for which such a language is not

intended. All the same, I can tell you this much: you are
aware that in the official science of today the role of the
observer becomes more and more important. Relativity,
the principle of indeterminacy, show the extent to
which the observer today intervenes in all these
phenomena. The secret of alchemy is this: there is a
way of manipulating matter and energy so as to produce
what modern scientists call 'a field of force'. This field
acts on the observer and puts him in a privileged
position *vis-á-vis* the Universe. From this position he
has access to the realities which are ordinarily hidden
from us by time and space, matter and energy. This is
what we call 'The Great Work'.

(Pauwels and Bergier 1968: 24)

Maybe alchemy knows another way of altering atomic structure
without the use of huge and costly nuclear reactors, and possibly there
are clues to this knowledge in the insistence on the almost endless
repetition of certain parts of the process, such as distilling and re-
distilling the liquid matter hundreds of times.

The philosophy of modern science could certainly now provide a
more hospitable climate for alchemical concepts. The world view has
grown; boundaries have been pushed back by the advent of new
branches of science, including quantum physics, which breaks down
the distinction between energy and matter, and demonstrates how the
'observer' is in reality a 'participator' in atomic experiments, affecting
the very particles that are worked on.

> Quantum theory thus reveals a basic oneness of the
> universe. It shows that we cannot decompose the world
> into independently existing smallest units. As we
> penetrate into matter, nature does not show us any
> isolated 'basic building blocks' but rather appears as a
> complicated web of relations between the various parts
> of the whole. These relations always include the
> observer in an essential way. The human observer
> constitutes the final link in the chain of observational
> processes, and the properties of any atomic objects can
> only be understood in terms of the object's interaction
> with the observer. This means that the classical ideal of
> an objective description of nature is no longer valid...

> In atomic physics, we can never speak about nature
> without, at the same time, speaking about ourselves.
>
> (Capra 1975: 71)

Quantum physics is not alone in bringing in ideas of consciousness, and of unity. 'Chaos theory' and its successors 'Complexity theory' and 'Emergence theory' opens out the possibility that one small action may have universal effects, and the concept of 'morphic resonance' (pioneered by Rupert Sheldrake in his 1981 book *A New Science of Life: The hypothesis of formative causation*) states that the individuals of a species are linked into a common field, which can both be influenced by the individual and can also transmit new knowledge to its members. Sheldrake's more recent work, extends this idea of the field of mind to include explanations for telepathy and 'the sense of being stared at'. (See Sheldrake 1999 and 2003.)

When the flexibility of time is also considered as part of human experience, then precognition also becomes a possibility within this theory, a concept tackled in depth in David Abram, *The Spell of the Sensuous* (Abram 1997).

Further theories will doubtless arise. Not all will stand up to the test, but what does seem to be happening is that there is increasing motivation to develop a world picture which can include not only physical materiality, but time, space and consciousness as well. The old rigid boundaries between mind and matter have crumbled. These new scientific premises are close to those upon which alchemy is based; hence alchemy may still be able to yield new scientific insights, for those who take the trouble to look.

Alchemy – where next?

Alchemy is still feeding the general culture of the Western world. We have seen how it continues to illuminate and inspire arts, human behavioural studies, and science. It throws light on pre-existent forms, such as music and poetry, and serves as fuel for creating new ones. However, these are spin-offs from alchemy, not the full practice of the tradition as it has been known. From this angle, we might say that alchemy is over; the elements of its practice, long-lived as they were, were subject to the conditions of time and society, conditions which have now dissolved.

Alchemical Sunrise: *a painting by Natalia Kapelyan-Danilin, 2000. Alchemy continues to provide a rich source of imagery for art and creative work in the contemporary world.*

Or does the spirit of alchemy go deeper even than the forms of alchemy as we know them? Traditions of knowledge weave their way quietly through aeons of cultural and religious change, and may change their outer forms so drastically that the continuity between one phase and the other is not recognised. The Kabbalah, for instance, known officially as a Judaic and Judaeo-Christian mystery tradition, may well be deeper rooted than its official history proclaims; the Tree of Life, its chief symbol and cosmic glyph, is found in strikingly similar forms both in Assyrian mythology and in Egyptian symbolism.

There is no doubt too that the symbols of alchemy live on, and many people find them a powerful tool both for self-transformation and for expanding knowledge about the dynamics of creation. In *Everyday Alchemy* I set out a method which follows a sequence of alchemical emblems as a way of engendering change within one's own alchemical vessel, the psyche, and as a way of exploring the miraculous possibilities of the universe that we inhabit. Even C.G. Jung, who was doubtful about the physical achievements of alchemy, accepted the possibility of miracles wholeheartedly, claiming that: 'Exceptions are just as real as probabilities. The premise of probability simultaneously postulates the existence of the improbable.' For him, 'a miracle is an archetypal situation which is accompanied by a corresponding emotion.' And we should not leave the emotion out of alchemy. Throughout the ages, alchemists have conducted their experiments with a sense of wonder and awe, and without that, alchemy turns into a cold and mechanistic practice, entirely at odds with its essential spirit.

The big question is then: What is alchemy? When all the outer forms are stripped away, what is left? If alchemy has to evolve a new form, it is from that underlying spirit that it will be fashioned. What can be discarded, without destroying the essence? Perhaps this essence cannot really be named; however, at its very simplest, the aim of alchemy is to transform base matter into gold. Now that we have reached the end of this particular survey of alchemy, it can readily be seen that this statement can be taken in many different ways. The future of alchemy may well depend on discovering yet another way in which it can be realised, perhaps something that, as yet, we can scarcely dream of.

Select bibliography

Key books for historical study:

C. A. Burland, *The Arts of the Alchemists,* Weidenfeld and Nicolson, 1967.

Garth Fowden, *The Egyptian Hermes: A historical approach to the late pagan mind*, Princeton University Press, 1986.

Timothy Freke and Peter Gandy, *The Hermetica: The lost wisdom of the pharaohs*, Piatkus, 1997.

Mark Haeffner, *A Dictionary of Alchemy*, Aquarian Press, 1991.

E.J. Holmyard, *Alchemy*, Pelican, 1957.

Jack Lindsay, *The Origins of Alchemy in Graeco-Roman Egypt,* Frederick Muller, 1970.

Charles Nicholl, *The Chemical Theatre,* RKP, 1980.

Alexander Roob, *Alchemy and Mysticism*, Taschen, 1997.

John Read, *Prelude to Chemistry*, G. Bell and Sons, 1936.

F. Sherwood Taylor, *The Alchemists,* Paladin, 1976.

Michael White, *Isaac Newton: The last sorceror*, Fourth Estate Ltd, 1997.

Alchemical texts – collections and single works:

Paul M. Allen, *A Christian Rosenkreutz Anthology,* Rudolf Steiner Publications, 1968.

Elias Ashmole, *Theatrum Chemicum Britannicum,* 1652 (reprinted 1967).

P.E.M. Berthelot, *Collection des Anciens Alchimistes Grecs.* Paris, 1888.

Johannes Fabricius, *Alchemy: The medieval alchemists and their royal art*, Diamond Books, 1994.

Cherry Gilchrist, *Everyday Alchemy: How to use the power of alchemy for daily change and transformation*, Rider, 2002.

N. Goodrick-Clarke, *Paracelsus: Essential Readings*, Crucible, 1990.

M. Maier, *Atlanta Fugiens*, trans. and ed. Joscelyn Godwin, Phanes Press, 1989.

Peter Marshall, *The Philosopher's Stone: A quest for the secrets of alchemy*, Pan Books, 2002.

Eirenaeus Philalethes, *Alchemical Works 1654–1683*, Cinnabar, 1994.

Jay Ramsay, *Alchemy: The art of transformation,*Thorsons, 1997.

Stanislas K. de Rola, *The Secret Art of Alchemy*, Thames and Hudson, 1973.

Trismosin, *Splendor Solis*, manuscript of 1682 translated Joscelyn Godwin, Phanes Press, 1991.

A.E. Waite (ed.), *The Hermetic Museum*, Elliott 1893.

Websites

www.levity.com hosted by Adam McLean is the leading website on alchemy, with a wealth of historical alchemical tracts and illustrations, and links to other useful alchemical websites and resources.

The author's website can be found at: www.cherrygilchrist.co.uk

Works cited

Abram, David, 1997, *The Spell of the Sensuous*, Vintage Books.

Allen, Paul M., 1968. *A Christian Rosenkreutz Anthology*, Rudolf Steiner Publications, New York

Ashmole, Elias, 1652, *Theatrum Chemicum Brittanicum* (reprinted Kessinger Publishing Company, no date)

Barbault, Armand, 1975, *Gold of a Thousand Mornings*, Spearman (translation of *L'Or du millie`me matin*. Editions Publications Premières, Paris, 1969).

Berthelot, P. E. M., 1888, *Collection des Anciens Alchimistes Grecs*.(Paris)

Boehme, Jacob, 1635, *The Signature of All Things* (*Signatura Rerum*) (reprinted James Clarke, 1969).

Capra, Fritjof, 1975, *The Tao of Physics*, Wildwood House.

Cockren, Archibald, 1940, *Alchemy Discovered and Restored*, Rider (reprinted by Health Research, California, 1963).

Dobbs, Betty, 1975, *The Foundations of Newton's Alchemy*, Cambridge UP.

Flamel, Nicolas, 1624, *Explanation of the Hieroglyphicall Figures*.

French, Peter, 1972, *John Dee*, RKP.

Geber (Jabir), 1928, *Works*, (ed. E. J. Holmyard), Dent.

Gilbert, R. A., 1983, *The Golden Dawn: Twilight of the Magicians*, Aquarian Press.

Godwin, Joscelyn, 1979, *Robert Fludd*, Thames and Hudson.

Works cited

Hopkins, A. J., 1967, *Alchemy: Child of Greek Philosophy*, AMS Press Inc.

Jung, C. G., 1963, *Memories, Dreams, Reflections*, Collins/RKP.

Jung, C. G., 1953, *Psychology and Alchemy*, RKP.

Jung, C.G., 1967, *Alchemical Studies*, RKP.

MacGregor Mathers, S.L. (trans.), 1970, *The Kabbalah Unveiled*, RKP.

McLean, Adam, 1979, 'The Birds in Alchemy', *The Hermetic Journal*, no. 5.

McLean, Adam, 1981a, 'Heinrich Khunrath', *The Hermetic Journal*, no. 12.

McLean, Adam, 1981b, 'Muller's Process', *The Hermetic Journal*, no. 12.

McLean, Adam, 1981c, 'Jacob Boehme', *The Hermetic Journal*, no. 14

Maier, Michael, 1617, *Atlanta Fugiens*, (translated and edited by Joscelyn Godwin, with accompanying cassette recording), Phanes Press 1989.

Martin, Luther H. (jun.), 1975, 'A History of the Psychological Interpretation of Alchemy', *Ambix* (March).

Needham, Joseph, 1956, *Science and Civilization in China*, Cambridge UP.

Needham, Joseph, 1968, *The Shorter Science and Civilization in China*, Cambridge UP.

Nicholl, Charles, 1980, *The Chemical Theatre*, RKP.

Norton, Thomas, 1477, *The Ordinall of Alchimy;* first published in English in Elias Ashmole, *Theatrum Chemicum Britannicum*, 1652.

Ouspensky, P. D., 1957, *The Fourth Way*, Knopp (reprinted Arkana 1986).

Pauwels, L. and Bergier, F., 1968, *The Morning of the Magicians*, Avon Books.

Paracelsus, 1894, *The Hermetic and Alchemical Writings of Aureolus Philippus Theophrastus Bombast, of Hohenheim, called Paracelsus the Great*, (ed. A. E. Waite), Elliott

Paracelsus, 1975, *Archidoxes of Magic*, Askin.

Powell, Neil, 1976, *Alchemy: The Ancient Science*, Aldus Books.

Ripley, George, 1591, *The Compound of Alchemy*.

Scott, Sir Walter (trans.), 1924, *Hermetica*; reprinted 1985 Shambhala.

Sheldrake, Rupert, 1981, *A New Science of Life: The hypothesis of formative causation*, Blond and Briggs.

Sheldrake, Rupert, 1999, *Dogs that know when their owners are coming home*, Hutchinson.

Sheldrake, Rupert, 2003, *The Sense of Being Stared At*, Hutchinson.

Shepperd, H.J., 1970, 'Alchemy: Origin or Origins?', *Ambix*, vol. 13 (July).

Stevens, Denis, 1980, *The Letters of Claudio Monteverdi*, Faber.

Strunk, Oliver, 1981, *Source Readings in Musical History, Vol. 3: The Baroque Era*, Faber

Sutherland, C. H. V., 1959, *Gold*, Thames and Hudson.

Taylor, A. M., 1966, *Imagination* and *the Growth of Science*, John Murray.

Taylor, F. Sherwood, 1976, *The Alchemists*, Paladin.

Thorndike, Lynn, 1923–58, A History of Magic and Experimental Science, Columbia UP.

Vaughan, Thomas, 1888, *The Magical Writings*, ed. A. E. Waite (reprinted Health Research, California, 1974).

Vaughan, Henry, 1976, *The Complete Poems*, Penguin.

Waite, A.E., (ed), 1893, *The Hermetic Museum*, Elliott.

Wilhelm, Richard (trans.), 1965, *The Secret of the Golden Flower*, RKP.

Works cited

Yates, Frances, 1964, *Giordano Bruno and the Hermetic Tradition*, RKP.

Yates, Frances, 1972, *The Rosicrucian Enlightenment*, RKP.

Yates, Frances , 1979, *The Occult Philosophy in the Elizabethan Age*, RKP.

Index

Entries in **bold** denote illustrations

Explore Fairy Traditions

Jeremy Harte

We are not alone. In the shadows of our countryside there lives a fairy race, older than humans, and not necessarily friendly to them. For hundreds of years, men and women have told stories about the strange people, beautiful as starlight, fierce as wolves, and heartless as ice. These are not tales for children. They reveal the fairies as a passionate, proud, brutal people.

Explore Fairy Traditions draws on legends, ballads and testimony from throughout Britain and Ireland to reveal what the fairies were really like. It looks at changelings, brownies, demon lovers, the fairy host, and abduction into the Otherworld. Stories and motifs are followed down the centuries to reveal the changing nature of fairy lore, as it was told to famous figures like W.B. Yeats and Sir Walter Scott. All the research is based on primary sources and many errors about fairy tradition are laid to rest.

Jeremy Harte combines folklore scholarship with a lively style to show what the presence of fairies meant to people's lives. Like their human counterparts, the secret people could kill as well as heal. They knew marriage, seduction, rape and divorce; they adored some children and rejected others. If we are frightened of the fairies, it may be because their world offers an uncomfortable mirror of our own.

'*Explore Fairy Traditions* is an excellent introduction to the folklore of fairies, and I would highly recommend it.' Paul Mason *Silver Wheel*

ISBN 978 1872 883 618. Published 2004. Demi 8vo (215 x 138 mm), 171 + vi pages, 6 line drawings, paperback. **£9.95**

Explore Mythology

Bob Trubshaw

Myths are usually thought of as something to do with 'traditional cultures'. The study of such 'traditional' myths emphasises their importance in religion, national identity, hero-figures, understanding the origin of the universe, and predictions of an apocalyptic demise. The academic study of myths has done much to fit these ideas into the preconceived ideas of the relevant academics.

Only in recent years have such long-standing assumptions about myths begun to be questioned, opening up whole new ways of thinking about the way such myths define and structure how a society thinks about itself and the 'real world'.

These new approaches to the study of myth reveal that, to an astonishing extent, modern day thinking is every bit as 'mythological' as the world-views of, say, the Classical Greeks or obscure Polynesian tribes. Politics, religions, science, advertising and the mass media are all deeply implicated in the creation and use of myths.

Explore Mythology provides a lively introduction to the way myths have been studied, together with discussion of some of the most important 'mythic motifs' – such as heroes, national identity, and 'central places' – followed by a discussion of how these ideas permeate modern society. These sometimes contentious and profound ideas are presented in an easily readable style of writing.

ISBN 978 1872 883 625. Published 2003. Perfect bound. Demi 8vo (215 x 138 mm), 220 + xx pages, 17 line drawings. **£9.95**

Also from Heart of Albion Press

Explore Folklore

Bob Trubshaw

**'A howling success, which plugs
a big and obvious gap'**

Professor Ronald Hutton

There have been fascinating developments in the study of folklore in the last twenty-or-so years, but few books about British folklore and folk customs reflect these exciting new approaches. As a result there is a huge gap between scholarly approaches to folklore studies and 'popular beliefs' about the character and history of British folklore. *Explore Folklore* is the first book to bridge that gap, and to show how much 'folklore' there is in modern day Britain.

Explore Folklore shows there is much more to folklore than morris dancing and fifty-something folksingers! The rituals of 'what we do on our holidays', funerals, stag nights and 'lingerie parties' are all full of 'unselfconscious' folk customs. Indeed, folklore is something that is integral to all our lives – it is so intrinsic we do not think of it as being 'folklore'.

The implicit ideas underlying folk lore and customs are also explored. There might appear to be little in common between people who touch wood for luck (a 'tradition' invented in the last 200 years) and legends about people who believe they have been abducted and subjected to intimate body examinations by aliens. Yet, in their varying ways, these and other 'folk beliefs' reflect the wide spectrum of belief and disbelief in what is easily dismissed as 'superstition'.

Explore Folklore provides a lively introduction to the study of most genres of British folklore, presenting the more contentious and profound ideas in a readily accessible manner.

ISBN 978 1872 883 601. Published 2002. Perfect bound, demi 8vo (215x138 mm), 200 pages, **£9.95**

Snake Fat and Knotted Threads

An introduction to traditional Finnish healing magic

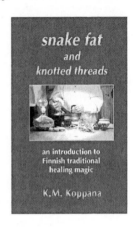

What did the Finnish cunning man carry in his magic pouch? How does one learn the language of the ravens? What is the Origin of the Cat? How do you attract a partner at Midsummer? These and much more are to be found in *Snake Fat and Knotted Threads*.

Snake Fat and Knotted Threads provides a unique resource about traditional Finnish healing magic and spells, folk customs and myths. All this detailed information is based on the author's research and practical experience.

> '*Snake Fat and Knotted Threads* is a rare and interesting book written by a woman who truly cares about the folk tradition of her own country. [...] In a world of 'Get Witch Quick' books and overcomplicated traditions, Koppana is refreshing... '
> Elswyth (on Wydways discussion list)

1st UK edition (revised from Finnish edition)

ISBN 978 1872 883 656. Published 2003. demy 8vo (215 x 138 mm), 83 + x pages, 13 b&w photos, 2 line drawings, paperback. **£7.95**

Myths of Reality

Simon Danser

'This liberal author's knowledge of contemporary society is amazingly broad. He exposits the mythic depths (and appearances) of everything from 'the myth of science' to superhero attitudes of contemporary American nationalism.

'Along the way he challenges many superficial trivialities about myths functioning in culture. He regards the mythic as a primary, highly effective agent of social ideology, and is never hesitant about demanding that the garments of our truly mythological capitalism are ill-fitting and socially harmful.

'This is the best book I know in terms of disclosing the pragmatic functioning of myth in society.'

William Doty, Professor Emeritus, The University of Alabama and author of
Mythography: The study of myths and rituals

Simon Danser asks us to think of myths as like the lenses in spectacles – we see the world through them, but rarely see them in their own right. He then systematically focuses on the myths at the core of the belief systems which create every aspect of what we take to be reality: religion, politics, commerce, science, knowledge, consciousness, self-identity, and much else that we take as 'given'.

This book reveals how reality is culturally constructed in an ever-continuing process from mythic fragments transmitted by the mass media and adapted through face-to-face and Internet conversations.

ISBN 978 1872 883 809. Published 2005. Demy 8vo (215 x 138 mm), 205 + xiv pages, paperback. **£12.95**

Heart of Albion

The UK's leading publisher of
folklore, mythology and cultural studies.

Further details of all Heart of Albion titles online at
www.hoap.co.uk

All titles available direct from Heart of Albion Press.

Please add £1.30 p&p (UK only; email
albion@indigogroup.co.uk for overseas postage).

To order books or request our current catalogue please contact

Heart of Albion Press

2 Cross Hill Close, Wymeswold
Loughborough, LE12 6UJ

Phone: 01509 880725
Fax: 01509 881715
email: albion@indigogroup.co.uk
Web site: www.hoap.co.uk